This book is a gift to you from Scottish Book Trust, a national charity changing lives through reading and writing, to celebrate Book Week Scotland (15–21 November 2021).

bookweekscotland.com

Celebration is a collection of true stories written by the people of Scotland. This book is one of 50,000 **free** copies – thank you for picking it up! If you enjoy it, help us share it with as many people as possible. Dip into it and share a few favourites with friends, display it, gift a copy to a partner, colleague or parent, or even leave it somewhere for a stranger to discover.
(We recommend a reading age of 15+.)

These stories are both funny and moving, paying tribute to the breadth of storytelling across multiple generations all over Scotland. We hope you enjoy them.

Happy reading!

#BookWeekScotland

A huge thank you to the following individuals who supported Scottish Book Trust as members of The Book Club

Christian Albuisson

Gordon Dalyell and Pamela Leslie

Lucy Juckes and Ben Thomson

Marian and Mark Deere

Martin Adam and William Zachs

Scott Lothian

and those who wish to remain anonymous

Celebration

scottishbooktrust.com

First published in 2021 by Scottish Book Trust, Sandeman House, Trunk's Close, 55 High Street, Edinburgh EH1 1SR

scottishbooktrust.com

The authors' right to be identified as an author of this book under the Copyright, Patents and Designs Act 1988 has been asserted

A CIP catalogue record for this book is available from the British Library

Typeset by Laura Jones

Printed and bound by CPI Group (UK) Ltd, Croydon CR0 4YY

Scottish Book Trust makes every effort to ensure that the paper used in this book has been legally sourced from well-managed and sustainable forests

Cover design by O Street

This is a free book, designed to be read alone or in groups, enjoyed, shared and passed on to friends. This book is gifted to you by Scottish Book Trust for Book Week Scotland 2021

Digital editions of this book are available from scottishbooktrust.com/celebration

Contents

Now that's worth celebrating

Here's to the good times

Family treasures

Quiet victories

*Stories by published authors.
Please be aware that this book is unsuitable for readers aged 14 or younger as it contains strong language and mature content.

Now that's
worth celebrating

50
Lynn Blair

I'm turning 50.

If you're 80 and reading this, you'll be rolling your eyes at the sheer nothingness of it. If you're 25 you probably can't even begin to imagine being my age. When I was 25, being 50 sounded old as hell. Time for a Parker pen, blood pressure tablets, the menopause and special kinds of holidays on large boats that contained hospitals. If I was lucky, I might still have some of my own teeth.

Now that I'm here of course, it's barely a thing. My foundations are the same as when I was 25. I'm still day-dreamy, lazy, rubbish at admin, a lover of learning, reading and swimming in cold water. But it wouldn't be 25 years well spent if I hadn't grown and learned a great deal. Fifty must mean more than being the butt of everyone's long-practised age jokes and the recipient of a bowel cancer screening test through the post. Best to ignore, then, the cultural expectations and instead look at what there is to really celebrate.

Because, surprisingly, there are many good things. Life is infinitely better than it was when you were 25. There's a whole chunk of wisdom and appreciation added on, not to mention a clear and defining sense of self. You say no and you mean it. You suspect you might have grown (whisper it) a bit difficult. This is faintly thrilling. Because you're less tolerant of nonsense, you don't fill silences. You don't hurry to answer, or laugh when it's not funny, but you're quick to mirth when it is. Perhaps you're sometimes a little rude to overly rehearsed sales people, but you need to save time. Chuggers take one look into your black, soulless eyes and don't even bother.

One bored afternoon during lockdown you cut off your long hair using cheap hairdressing scissors and your husband's clippers. It felt better instantly. You've got a bleach blonde pixie now, all home-made and punky, and are vain enough to be happy that you have to deal with dark roots. You still love ugly space princess shoes that everyone pulls horrified faces at and you have been known to sit in the front row at the ballet wearing your slippers. You've always been a bit Jenny Joseph, but now you're revving up and growing into it. There's a red lipstick in every pocket (damn you, facemasks). Bras must not have an underwire and you have strong feelings about knicker-shapes and necklines. Tailoring rocks – provided it's worn with serious trainers and a T-shirt – and you know what you love so well that you can cast a sweeping eye around a shop, dismiss all of it and move on in less than a minute.

There is no chance that you will spend three figures on a handbag or a pair of shoes, but on books, concerts or holidays you're prepared to be generous. Money and you have made an uneasy peace. The savings account gets money paid in monthly and you know what's in it and what it's for. You're not rich, but you're free and that, as the years have shown you, is worth more than lots of cash. Out of character, you turn a blind eye to the price of that perfume you love because you're nothing if not contradictory. The constant pursuit of new and better objects does not impress, and you choose your people accordingly. New books and new plants matter. New kitchens and couches do not.

3

Somehow, by thinking and noticing, you've managed to pull off the magic trick of getting out of your own way. This is an age-induced superpower: a total belief in action and moving things forward physically, even if your brain is determinedly stuck in some way. You talk to yourself kindly, encouragingly even, and that means your mind is a gentle, calm and pleasant place to be. Just do something, you tell yourself: it'll work, it always does. The discouraging voice –sometimes editor, sometimes critic – is largely silent these days, pensioned off as this restructuring took place. How you wish you could gift a gentle internal voice to the 25-year-olds.

And the really good bits? You've been married to the same man for twenty years and you still adore him, often and completely. Birthing suites, deathbeds and several washing machines later, there are no inhibitions. Love is perfectly efficient and if you don't think efficient is a romantic word now, wait until you've less time in front of you with the love of your life, than behind. Bodies, with their imperfect and damaged landscapes, are celebrated and enjoyed, and arguments last half the time because you've had them before and they were pointless then too. The background is all filled out, leaving the two of you free to play on the stage. Your kids are getting bigger and you're doing a good job: they're happy and kind and funny. You have a home: messy and busy, and full of love and cake and humour. The van you drive is ancient, so muddy feet or sea-soaked swim-suited bottoms don't matter. Work is just work and you're glad of it, but it's not where your real life is. At 25 you could not have acknowledged the truth in that.

Write down the number 50: it's solid, curvy and dependable. It knows the value of a good lunch. You have a suspicion – which you'll need years to prove – that

50 is the last number that calls to itself as if it matters. It's the final wall that you break through and on the other side is a world where you're just a person, not an age, not a judgement, not a list of things achieved. No one expects anything much of you now because – well, you're 50. And that, my friends, is the real essence of your celebration. Because now, as a fully formed, anonymous adult, you can finally get started.

Author note: *I am turning 50 this year, and surprisingly, I'm really happy about that. I hope my writing strikes a chord with both those who are young and think 50 is old, and those who are old, who think I'm a spring chicken!*

Running For It
Louise Baillie

There's a fire burning inside me. It stretches from the bottom of my chest and rises out through my mouth in ugly, breathless pants. Sweat drips from my forehead onto my front, turning the light blue of my T-shirt a deep shade of navy. My legs are squealing in protest but still I push them on. You can do this, a forceful voice yells from inside my head. Don't give up, it encourages. It offers a counter message to every other part of my body that is telling me to stop.

With every step I take, I am closer to my goal. My legs move on automatic pilot as if they know there's a job to be done and are intent only on finishing it. My surroundings pass by in a blur of greens and browns because I am only focused on going forwards. Nearly there, that voice calls out again. Who is this motivator that has climbed inside my head?

The air is thick and clammy. Was it really this warm earlier in the day? It is as though I am fighting my way through the stuffiness, arms flailing, legs stomping. It is just another hurdle in this self-inflicted race. Come on, the voice inside roars, as my end-point comes into view.

It isn't far. A few metres. You're nearly there! The voice is like a thousand spectators at a sports match. The fire inside rages. My legs wail in defeat. Then, as I stumble over the finish line, it all comes to a startlingly abrupt end. I imagine a ribbon torn in half by the body that stumbles through it. The crowd cheers. The commentators yell. In reality, an oblivious dog walker is the only witness to my accomplishment. They walk on, swerving by the sweaty body on the pavement.

My body feels an immediate release as the pace slows and I grind to a halt. I wipe the sweat from my forehead and grab air in thick, greedy mouthfuls. I stop to crouch on the ground even though every coach I've met has said this is the worst thing to do after a race. It's over, but have I done it? I look at my watch. It has stopped precisely on the 5-kilometre benchmark and flashes 25 minutes 38 seconds in big, bold numbers. A personal best.

It's an ordinary Tuesday night when I pull off my greatest running feat, but it has taken three years of Tuesday night runs to bring me to this point. What once started as a way to release pent-up energy from a 9–5 job turned into a passion, and then an obsession, as I found ways to push my body step by forceful step. Like a compulsory runner's to-do list, I checked off the 10k, the half-marathon and the coaching qualification. Now, though, all I crave is speed.

The first time I put on my trainers and dashed out the front door for a jog, I was oblivious to the commitment I was about to make. On that first journey, I made it to the end of a nearby street before coming to a breathless stop. The idea of PBs and races seemed foreign – for someone else to invest in but not at all for me. Yet, Tuesday after Tuesday, I put in jog after jog and suddenly those goals didn't seem so alien. Gradually, I even came to call myself a runner.

Now a huge grin settles on my face as the scale of my accomplishment settles in. Whoever coined the phrase 'runner's high' was not wrong. My elation, I imagine, matches what any drug could offer. I almost laugh out loud with happiness, stopping only out of fear that I might get some concerned looks from passers-by. As I slowly win back my breath, the voice inside calls out again. You did it, it says, calmer now.

I ease myself up off the ground and begin to stretch off my legs. I pull at my hamstrings and my calves, easing out the tension that has built up in the last 30 minutes. I move slowly and with care, appreciative of my body and all that it's managed to do tonight. As I move, I watch another runner approach in the distance. The steady thud of their footsteps and the pained expression on their face becomes sharper as they gradually get closer. When they pass by, I offer an enthusiastic grin. Maybe it will help them through. Maybe, I think to myself, this little gesture of encouragement will see them through to a personal best.

Lazily, I begin the jog back to my house. I am a different runner now that the fire has been doused and the main goal complete. I plod by great elm and oak trees. I glance in the windows of quiet homes. Now that I finally have my breath back, I even exchange greetings with other people out enjoying this mild Tuesday night. Soon, I am back at my front door and I swing it open, announcing my presence with a new burst of energy.

'How was your run?' comes the call from inside, and I grin.

'I got a PB!' I yell back excitedly.

Author note: *Running has brought me a lot of joy and reason for celebration over the past few years, but this evening was a reminder that we don't always need fancy running events or big races in order to make significant gains in the sport. Sometimes the biggest accomplishments can come on an ordinary Tuesday night.*

Bloom
Ali MacDougall

Please note: this piece contains descriptions some readers may find upsetting.

She was shrivelling like a rose without water after he died. Washing, eating and sleeping were things she had done then. When he was here. Not now. Raggle-headed she wandered to the wood with their dog, whose ears went down when she screamed and wept. He stayed close, the spring in his step gone.

All suggestions fell flat. Medication made things worse. Therapists seemed to say the wrong things. The health service had nothing else to offer the endlessness of her grief. Friends fell away, no canoe trips or dips in the river at Abbey St Bathans this year. Just nothing. The bright little dog wanted walks and she dutifully met his needs, in the woods or at the beach.

One day they swam together, his little legs paddling hard to keep up with her as they struck out through the waves near the harbour. She felt different in the sea. The salty coldness blocked out her grief and she felt a wholeness as every body system adapted to the new environment. She felt waves, tides and seaweed enfold her and carry her along. She went again. The tide was out and she had to go beyond the harbour to swim. Toppers were heading to Craigleith, their sails flapping wildly. A couple told her she was bonkers from the harbour wall. She felt alive and kept powering through.

9

Swimming days were better. She realised there were little chunks of time that hadn't been occupied with thoughts of him, how he died, why he died, what she could have done differently. Swimming days required a good breakfast. Hot chocolate. A nice warm shower.

A friend joined her, full of trepidation and fear of the cold. Together they shivered on the beach, her friend watching in awe as she strode off, waded in and went under with a primal scream. 'Come on!' she yelled.

Her friend gingerly paddled in. It was beyond shocking. She wanted to turn and run to the car but the face peeking out from between the waves and the voice commanding, 'One, two three,' urged her in and under. Extremes of cold and exhilaration hit her. It was fabulous. Three strokes and out. To the towel, her coat, the car, home, skin red and mind glowing.

Six months since that day. Both women have bloomed. The shrivelled rose has flowered again, her batteries recharged with wave power, she is coping with her loss and enjoying her own company. The tired friend has grown new shoots; feels rejuvenated and energised; is loving her new relationship with the sea and the surf forecast.

The now almost daily trips to the harbour, the catch-up on the details of each other's lives, the half-hour swim. The discovery one day, halfway across the bay, that 50 years ago their mothers, at opposite ends of the planet, had prepared grapefruit in exactly the same way made them laugh all the way to the other side. The restorative flask of cocoa. The repetition of an experience that is never the same twice.

It's food for the soul. It makes us bloom.

Author note: *My friend was desolate after her partner died. I have never seen grief like it and sometimes it seemed like there was no way to get through to her. I noticed a difference the first day she swam with the dog. It was like she was in charge of something, instead of being controlled by grief. When she invited me to join her, it was the first positive statement she had made since he'd died, and although I didn't fancy the North Sea in October, I gave it a shot. Glad I did.*

A Sealabration
Rachael Crofts

It was my best friend Jenny who started all of this! She was the real inspiration. She's travelled the world doing animal conservation work and now spends her days on a boat looking for whales, dolphins, sea birds and seals. She's incredible.

I, on the other hand, work in an office. I'd always been interested in the work she does so when she texted me to say there was a Marine Mammal Medic course taking place in the summer in my small town, I thought I'd take a gamble and give it a go.

Don't get me wrong, I was scared. I'd never done anything like this before. I had to buy a wetsuit. Then I had to buy another one after having to be peeled, unceremoniously, out of the first by my husband and blushing dad.

I attended the course, and the usual round of introductions followed. I was in the company of experienced divers, vets, marine biologists and environmental conservationists. My nerves weren't eased when I had to say, 'Hi, I'm Rachael, I work in HR and have never even been snorkelling.'

Anyway, I completed the course and felt proud at the end to say I was now a qualified Marine Mammal Medic with the British Divers Marine Life Rescue (BDMLR). It wasn't until Christmas Day when my parents gave me a beautiful silver dolphin charm for my bracelet that I felt a pang of guilt. I'd done some fundraising for them but hadn't attended any of the call-outs. If I was being honest, I felt like a fraud.

Boxing Day, and a call-out comes in: a seal needs help. Could this be my chance? I was terrified but called Jenny and she talked me through what I'd need to do. I psyched myself up and eventually offered to attend but with all my procrastinating someone had beaten me to it. I felt a bit relieved. At least I'd been willing to go; I'd call that progress.

December 27th, and it happens again. I get the call and before I've had time to panic, I volunteer and am picked to go.

A young seal pup had been picked up across the border and needed driven to the rescue centre in Alloa for rehabilitation. I was an Uber driver for a seal. I drove to the meeting point and got there first. As I waited for the other car to arrive, the nerves really crept in.

Eventually they arrived, and we awkwardly transferred the strangest passenger to ever ride in my car from theirs to my own. A 4-week-old pup with a mottled coat. He was still clinging to his adorably cute, white fluff, which they usually lose around three weeks old. He looked up at me with big, sad, dark eyes and I could see they were dry – he was dehydrated, so the race was on to get him the medical attention he needed.

On the journey, I spoke softly to him. In hindsight this was as much for my benefit as for his as I tried to stay calm and reassure us both that everything would be okay. The roads were terrible. The blizzard whipped at my windscreen as I made the unfamiliar journey.

As I arrived, one of the rescue volunteers greeted us and together we carried the seal in his crate through to be weighed. I tried my best not to react to the thick, fishy air that hit me as I nervously followed their lead to a small room they'd prepared for his arrival.

A towel was laid out for him as if he were a holidaymaker, and a heat lamp cast a rosy glow in the stark, white, concrete room. He was scared and didn't seem keen on his new abode. He wouldn't budge from his crate until eventually we had to unceremoniously tip him out like a failed cake mix plopping into the bin. I took a photo of him, finally safe and settled, to share with the other Marine Mammal Medics. It was a sad photo really. You could see the outline of his shoulders and hips, not something you should ever see of these famously round and clumsy creatures.

Each season there's a theme for naming the seals, and this time it was board games. As it was my first rescue, I was delighted when they said I could name him. I called him Dobble – a family favourite of ours. The drive home went by in a blur. I was filled with a mix of adrenaline and worry about whether Dobble would make it. One of the toughest parts is that the rescue centre is too busy to provide updates, so you just have to cross your fingers and hope for the best. And that's what I did.

A few months later, I got my second call-out. This time, a different character entirely to the timid and subdued Dobble. This one was stinky, loud and very stubborn. He had a lot of fight in him, as I could tell from his snappy teeth as well as the cuts to his brow and eyes, probably sustained from a tussle with some rocks in the stormy seas.

I made the same journey, a bit more familiar this time. After the weigh-in and the drop-off, I was on my way out when we heard a scuffle and raised voices. The volunteer and I went to see if we could help and found a seal charging down the wet corridor. I jumped out of the way, as three workers cornered him with a broom and wrestled him into his weigh-in bag.

'Sorry about that,' one lady said. 'That's Dobble, he's a bit of a feisty one'.

I couldn't help but laugh. I hadn't recognised him with his smart adult coat and all his lovely chub. He was strong and healthy and now I was the one who was afraid of him.

Author note: *I was inspired by a series of events that took me far out of my comfort zone and ultimately had a happy ending for all involved.*

Celebration in Recovery
Matthew Gallacher

I came to Phoenix House after 36 years of drugs, crime and prison. I've counted as the years went by, almost 27 years in prison, all over Great Britain. I punished my body with drug addiction.

It is a selfish disease. My family suffered. It's remarkable I am sat here alive today. Not just jail but treatment centres all over Britain. My very first rehab was a place called 'Inward House', which was in Lancaster.

I had been released from Wymott Prison near Leyland, Lancashire. I was supposed to go to Inward House on the day of release. Instead, I went to Morecambe Bay and got heroin and temazepam sleepers.

I arrived there the next day and said I hadn't used drugs! It turned out they were asking would I take a drugs test. So, I was lying straight away. I'd gone there to change, and I was already lying to them. I was there three months. I decided to leave in August of 1997.

So, I packed my stuff and sneaked out, only to go to a doctor and get 28 yellow Valium. It was the biggest mistake I ever made. So, years and years of prison time have taken their toll on me.

The community here is tremendous.

The support I have is so valuable. But inevitably, the health issues I have are the price of 36 years of addiction. The prize at the end of my time will be massive. Never have I managed to stay drug free.

The support I have here and outside is going to be so important. I am 52 years old, and I hope by my 53rd birthday to be clean.

'God grant me the serenity to accept the things I cannot change, courage to change the things I can and wisdom to know the difference.'

Mr Wales
Ross Sayers

Mr Wales was my high school English teacher. He was a great man and, if you'll forgive the cliché of an author talking about how important his high school English teacher was to him, I'd like to share a few memories I have of him.

I will be referring to my teacher as Mr Wales. Because that's how I knew him. Because that's what I called him when I stuck my hand up in class and asked for help. Because, even though I am now 29, I still feel a bit awkward calling him Colin. (He was a TEACHER, how disrespectful of me to call him by his name!)

Mr Wales was a constant for me throughout high school. He was my English teacher in first year, when I used to sit in his room, struggling to pay attention, because the girl I really fancied sat right in front of me. He was my English teacher in sixth year, where I just about managed a C in Advanced Higher (and struggled to pay attention because the girl I really fancied was also in this class).

Mr Wales taught me about books, about language, and how to convey myself through my words. He taught me *Romeo and Juliet, Death of a Salesman* and *Lord of the Flies*. He told me I should read *Guards! Guards!* by Terry Pratchett because I'd love it (and he was right). Years later, my very first attempt at a novel would be a poor effort at trying to replicate the humour and fantasy of the Discworld books.

Mr Wales also taught us Media Studies. As you can

imagine, the idea of getting to watch films in school (not just on the last days of term) was too exciting an opportunity to pass up. It was in Mr Wales's room that I watched *Jaws* for the first time. It was in Mr Wales's room that I watched *It's a Wonderful Life* for the first time. It was in Mr Wales's room that I started crying while watching *It's a Wonderful Life* for the first time.

One thing that films and real life have in common is this: teachers are inspirational. The difference between the two, however, is that in real life, it isn't always obvious how inspiring something or someone is. In films, there are clues. The music swells. The camera moves to a close-up of the hero. Textbooks are ripped up. Ties are thrown in the air. Days are seized, etc.

In real life, there are no moments like this. Teachers don't build to one giant, incredible, life-defining moment of inspiration which totally shapes their students for the rest of their lives. Instead, they have a million little moments like this, year upon year.

The inspiring moment a teacher provides is not cinematic. It's something simple, mundane. It's the pat on the shoulder when you're upset and trying to hide it. It's the smiley face and the 'this is great work!' scrawled in nearly illegible handwriting at the top of your essay. It's the moment you find out your teacher likes a band that you like and you realise that maybe they have a life outside the walls of the school.

So when I look back, I find I cannot identify a definitive moment where Mr Wales made me realise I could become a writer. Because there was no big moment. (I didn't even do any writing back then, I figured that was something only grown-ups could do.) But what I can identify are the little moments when he made me feel I was someone better than I believed I was.

In first year, when he told me he liked *The Young Ones* poster I'd covered my jotter in. In fourth year, when I got the first and, as it turned out, only 25/25 mark for an essay (I spent around five hours on it at home, far more than the allotted hour I should've had in class). In sixth year, when I told him how much I'd enjoyed *Guards! Guards!* and how I'd already ordered the follow-up, *Men at Arms*.

I wanted to impress, Mr Wales. I wanted to be someone that he considered a friend, a peer. He made me want to be the best version of myself I could be.

Mr Wales will live on, like all great teachers, in the hearts of everyone who was lucky enough to be taught by him. Most likely because his favourite thing to do, just as the lesson was coming to an end, just as the room was quiet enough and none of us were prepared, was to bellow at the top of his voice:

'OH MY GOD,' gesturing to the clock, 'IS THAT THE TIME?!'

This goes through my head on a daily basis, and I bet I'm not the only one from Bannockburn High who can say that.

I think one of the tragedies of growing up is realising that you will never be able to repay your favourite teachers. Because you didn't realise what they were doing at the time. Back then, if I had been asked why my teachers chose to go into teaching, I probably would've answered that it was because they hated children so much. Now I can see the opposite is true. Teachers are a special breed. They know that they will very likely receive no word of thanks at the end of a lesson. And they do it anyway, because they know what we're like. We're just kids. And someday we'll grow out of it.

Thank you, teachers.

Thank you, Mr Wales.

Celebrate
Elle McNicoll

It may be because of what makes me different but it always takes a little bit of time to realise that something monumental has happened. That a milestone has been met or an achievement realised. Part of being neurodivergent means processing things at a different speed to the average person. Birthdays are sometimes difficult to take in or enjoy. Too busy trying to make eye contact with every guest. Making sure that I'm making the right faces and performing correctly. It's a sensory bombardment and I'm usually too busy focusing on other people to process and digest what is happening. It's not until a few days later, when I've finally returned to my version of calm, that I remember the things to celebrate.

Without dwelling on the obvious reasons why this last year has been different from those that came before, I have been able to recognise one thing.

A year that was terrible in so many ways became the year that everything in my life changed and I was able to celebrate something that was hidden for 26 years before.

Having my debut novel published is certainly something to celebrate. It's a monumental achievement. That's something that I need to remind myself sometimes. Writing and finishing a book is an act that deserves celebration, even if its fate is to sit in a drawer and never be read. Writing a book is difficult. Doubt and life often get in the way. So its completion alone is something to celebrate, and it earns you the title of 'writer'.

Publication is a whole other journey. Decisions about your work are made without you, some things move quickly while other things take months. Surviving the publication process is also something to celebrate. The night before your book is sent out into the world, the full reality hits. People are actually going to read your words.

That feeling alone is often frightening enough to keep me from my desk (my figurative desk, I can't afford a real one just yet).

However, it was through writing and publishing my first novel that I came to my epiphany. Albeit slowly.

I was fulfilling my obligations to promote my book. When I signed my contract I knew I was signing with an incredible publisher. Wonderfully committed, but a small press. So I was comfortable in the knowledge that my book would not be strewn across supermarket shelves. It would not embark on a grand tour of the world. It would not sell to other territories or be made into a film or television show. It would not win awards or be written about in the newspaper. I would be lucky to get a small band of readers and see my book in the occasional library.

I was perfectly happy with that. For one reason.

In announcing my book to the world, I was also announcing something else. Something equally personal. Something deeply private, up until then.

I was announcing that I am neurodivergent. Something only a few people knew. Some doctors, some loved ones. While I have spent my life hearing, 'there's something wrong with you, isn't there?', I don't actually count that as them 'knowing' that I am neurodivergent.

Now, the Advance Information sheet told people that my book was written by a neurodivergent author.

At the time I thought, 'This is okay. It's a small book climbing an uphill battle which will probably be read by less than 100 people. One hundred people knowing is nothing. It's totally fine.'

I continued to celebrate that my little book was going to find its little audience. A pandemic arriving a couple of months before its release saddened me but also settled my nerves about people learning the truth.

I had to state that I am neurodivergent, so my community would know that the book came from truth and experience. It was for them, nobody else.

Publication day would be met with virtual celebrations at home.

But when the book was published, everything started to change.

Things started to happen, things that I knew I should celebrate. The book was made Children's Book of the Week in both *The Times* and *The Sunday Times*. It was well reviewed. It sold out in online retail spaces. A school revealed that they had bought 300 copies. It was made Book of the Month by both Blackwell's and Waterstones. It was announced that a publisher in New York wanted to bring out an American edition.

Suddenly, without fully realising what I had done, I was exposed. It was not hundreds of people who now knew my once most private secret. It was thousands. It was printed in newspapers.

Messages came flooding in. Most of them beautiful. People who related to the book, who had found paragraphs too close to the bone. They quoted my words back to me, from the book and from interviews. They thanked me. They shared their stories. I treasured it.

But there were other messages. Messages telling me that I'm an abomination. That I should never celebrate the fact that I am, in their words, broken.

It was conflicting. And lonely.

The book's success continued and in March 2021, I found myself in the *Blue Peter* studio, about to accept an award. It was live television. The change in routine, the unfamiliarity, the level of social masking required was weighing on me. It was hard in a sensory way. The lights and sound were very intense. It's not something you can change, just something you have to accept.

As I was standing behind the set, waiting to go on live to collect the award, everything hit me. I didn't have to hide anymore. Yes, there are people who are prejudiced. Yes, there are abusers. But there is also acceptance and love.

I heard myself say the words,

'I am a neurodivergent author.'

And I celebrate that. I'm proud of that. I will never hide from that again.

I will never hide from anyone again.

Stories and Self
Jacqueline Boland

Although we've been locked down, I have travelled.

I've tasted the sticky sweetness of candy floss
and drifted towards the smell of fresh popcorn at a
mysterious circus in the secret hours of night. I've
gazed upon shimmering spires of glass, cities soaked in
starlight and ancient kingdoms long since lost. I've felt
the weightlessness of floating through whorls of galaxies
and the blistering skin from traipsing tirelessly through
sun-scorched deserts. I've encountered thieves and
pirates, befriended fae and witches, saved princes and
mermaids. I have felt more, more, more than ever.

Although we've been locked down, I have opened up.

Bloomed as the flowers in spring from a seed buried
deep and forgotten. Abandoned. Now watered with words
spilling from the pages of books, endless books. Fed with
imagination, dreams and more words but bursting from
within, begging to be released into the world. Stories
demanding to be told. Dreams waiting to be realised.
Every root is a part of myself I'd forgotten existed,
tangling in the soil and taking purchase. Every sprouting
petal is an idea, an opportunity, a part of myself I could
be, waiting to be released in a whisper of wind.

Remember this, it says. When the world is loud again
and all your distractions have returned, remember what
it was to dream.

Although we've been locked down, we've found time.

The time to think, to feel, to reflect. The time to knit,
to paint, to bake banana bread. The time to reconnect

– with others, with nature, with ourselves. The time to read and write and create and chase long-forgotten dreams. Every project and procrastination, odd-job and hobby – every time we said 'one day', well, that 'one day' arrived. If not now, when? When will we ever have a time like this again? The time to be. Just, be.

Although we've been locked down, I've found myself. I've rediscovered the little girl who loved words – drinking them in, soaking them up and rearranging them into something new. A dream of writing stories, chewed up and devoured by fear, resurfacing after reading again like I once did as a child with all the time in the world. In the year that never was, I've remembered how to enjoy my own company, how to slow down and be still and be comfortable doing so. I've come face to face with the little girl and vowed I will not forget her again.

Words. Such delicate little things with such immeasurable impact. The unimaginable power of words plucked carefully for purpose and placed on a page, or stirred into a frenzy from our hearts and passionately spoken aloud – to comfort, to empower, to upset, to bring joy and to connect. There's not been much to talk about, but I can talk about books. I haven't been able to see my family and friends, but I can write them letters. I can't comfort a friend over a coffee or with a hug, but I can send them a message to let them know I'm here.

And I am grateful. This time, for me, has been a celebration of stories and self. Whether it's the book you curl up with to escape to another world, the rise of voices that will be silenced no longer, the truth that always emerges in time, or what we tell ourselves to make sense of our lives. Each and everything is a story and we all have one to tell. And what do I want mine to be? A story isn't a story until it's shared – do I dare dip into the ink?

Author note: *I always said that writing a novel was something I would do 'one day', but life gets in the way. I started obsessively reading again at the start of lockdown, which reignited my dream of writing creatively. This is the first step in my journey of acknowledging it and giving it a go.*

Here's to the good times

Gordon's Waddin
Harry

Glasgow, December 2019

Ah wis staundin ootside the Blythswood Square Hotel, of all places, hauvin a cheeky fag and mindin mah ain business, waitin fur the lads tae saunter o'er an' get this waddin done wi. Spoilin' the silence, Big Magz hookies up, sparkin a Mayfair Super King and keekin up at the dreich sky.

'It's no gonnae be a white waddin then, is it?' she says.

'Nah, he's aff it.'

'Whit?'

'Whit?'

'Are you bein wide?' She glowers at me like ah've tried to nick her battered sausage.

'Eh…' ah says, always feart tae get a doin' aff Big Magz. Yeh ne'er really ken how much she kens. 'Oh, there's the troops noo.' It wisnae Hampden Cars but the Almichty, sendin his angels in a Skoda tae save ma bahookie.

'Oi oi oi!' Baldy Steve says as he stammies oot the motor. Paul an' Johnnie in the back seat are jaked an aw'. Wouldnae hauv expectit anything less fae they lot than a roll an' Bucky fur thir breakfast.

Steve bolts up the stair and rubs his haunds taegither against the baltic weather, pauchlin a squatch inside as his puss turns.

'Jesus, she's a bit orange, int she?'

'That's Gordon's sister,' Magz says tae him, no turnin' around.

'Guid thing we're no hauvin this waddin in a chapel,

ay? She'd need permission fae the polis tae march aroond looking like tha'.'

Big Magz taps her fag aff, no impressed wi any of these wallopers. Ah dinny blame her, tae be honest.

'Way-hay!' Paul shouts tae hauf the toon as the motor speeds aff. 'Budapest, man! Buda-fu... Oh, hiya Magz, ah didny see you there.'

'I'll didny see you! Yeh haverin bampot. Mah Gordon came back fae that trip wi bloody pneumonia. I telt youse boys tae keep him fae makin an erse ae hisel.'

'It wiz minus ten, Magz,' Paul says. As if we all didny stoat aboot Buda, Pest an every scheme in between wi nae jaekets in sight.

'Aye, it wis awfy cauld there,' Steve says. 'An anyway, Magz, he prolly just haud the clap.'

'Youse are a right bunch ae reprobates,' Magz says, flickin the end of her fag intae the foggy yonder. 'Apart fae you, Johnnie, you're the guid wan.'

'It's funny,' Johnnie says, strikin a riddy, 'ah only met Gordon at his first waddin.' He keeks at me, as if it wis ma fault.

'That wis tae Fraser, aye?' Paul asks. 'Wis way before ma time.'

'Aye,' ah says, 'A guid few year ago noo. They done it the day aefter wee Nicola brought it in.'

'Oor Gordon's a right lad's lad, int he?' Steve says, howfin oan his vape. 'Twa waddins an ah'm still waitin oan ma first winch!'

'Is ye, aye?' Magz says, smilin fur once in her life like the mither of the bride should. 'Fraser wisnae his first waddin.' She sparks anither Super King while Steve's face droops.

'Yer aff yer heid.'

'Ah'm certainly no, sunshine.'

Steve sees me grinnin and glowers fur an answer. Whit wi me bein the high heedjin on aw hings Gordon-related.

'Aye, it's true,' ah says. 'Back in 2008, mibbe 2009. He'd met some American boy who'd come o'er tae the uni. Some mad architect. They got merrit at City Hall in that New York, so's they did.'

'Aye, it wis magic,' Magz agrees, sookin oan her fag. Ah don't hink she ever forgave Gordon fur dumpin a minted yank.

'It wis quality, aye,' ah says tae the lads' soor coupons. 'A whole gang ae us flew over. The troops cuttin' aboot Times Square wi bottles ae Mad Dug. Mind, Magz, we found that wee shop wi Irn Bru and Tunnock's Tea Cakes? Bought the lad oot ae aw his stock.'

'Mental. When did he get divorced?' Johnnie asks.

'Eh. . .' ah keek at Magz, who shrugs. 'Ah dunno, tae no tell ye a lie.'

'Aye,' she says. 'So mind yer gubs in case the registrar overhears.' She flicks her fag forrit. 'Right, boys, Magz is gaspin fur a bevy. Ah'm no gonnae sit through anither hoofter waddin wiout bein blootered.'

Only Johnnie's shocked. Unfamiliar wi the ways o' Big Magz.

'I'll take you in, doll.' Steve grabs her arm and they daunder inside. 'Ah'm only here fur the stovies anyhoo.'

Johnnie stays oot wi me, footerin wi his tie, aw nervous like he's aboot tae ask fur a massive tap.

'Whit ye been up tae?' ah says.

'Hee haw. How's the gaff?'

'Same as it wis when ye went an done a sly flittin when ah wis at ma work.'

'Aw rite Harry, calm doon, ah'm only askin.'

'An ah'm only tellin.' Ah spark up anither fag fur want ae sumfin else tae say. 'Hink you an Andy will be next?'

'Me an Andy gettin merrit? You're aff yer heid. Ma da dusnae even hauv a scooby aboot him, fur wan hing.'

'Your da?' ah says, no understaundin. 'But ah ken yer da. Me an yer da wir pals.'

'Aye, but he dusnae ken Andy's a big ragin' tim.'

'Ah.'

'Naw, if we ever dae sumfin it wilnae be aw this palava. Doon tae Gretna fur the day and pick up a munchy box oan the way hame.'

'Thank God you telt me tae sling ma hook, Johnnie.'

'Aye, ah mind you're too guid fur a munchy box, you are. Or at least ye hink so. Funny,' Johnnie says, as if we wis staundin in the steamie an no freezin oor diddies aff, 'ye stert tae hink yer sumfin after comin oot. Bein yersel an aw, but then folk like Gordon pop up an show yeh you've been dain it wrang the whole time.'

'Aye, wir no as fandabby as we hink, whit wi Gordon scadgin a third wan.'

'An bein a bigamist, mare like.'

'Or a trigamist.'

'That's oor Gordon.'

Author note: *This is a story about attending a friend's wedding at the end of 2019, not knowing it would be the last one for a long time. It harks back to the casual freedom we used to take for granted at times of celebration. Sharing gossip with friends and family. It looks forward to a time when we'll be able to celebrate again, surrounded by the people who make up the stories of our lives.*

Revelry
Open Book Creative Writing Group

Don't just invite your friends. Ask the person who
weighs on your heart.
Request sunshine and an absence of wasps.
The day opens nervously.
The first thing to do is to decide what to make.
Make a list.
Gather the wee ones and bribe with secrets.
Remember matches.
The barbecue won't light.
Panic.
People arrive.
Revelry is compulsory.
Banquet on the here and now.
The whole extravaganza begins over and over and over
again.
It's an adventure.
Keep singing.

To the Good Times
Daniel Shand

It'll be a long time comin, that first visit. We're no sure where or when it'll happen, just that it will. We're no sure where or when, but we ken exactly how it'll go, how it'll look, how it'll feel. But first things first: we'll havetae agree a day. We'll havetae see who's working when, see when we're aw available, get everythin sorted.

The day of, we're gonnae be ready far too early. We're gonnae pace between windows till it's time for the bus or train or whatever, an we'll aw be doin the same, wherever we are. We will walk the street, comin in fae various locations, an as we go, we'll feel a wee touch sick, nervy for no reason at aw; mair excitement than nerves, but it'll feel close. An ye wouldnae call it a skip in the step exactly, but oor trainers, clean fae lack a use, will move light on the pavements. It'll be warm too, ideally; we'll no have jackets on. Everythin necessary'll be in bags or jeans; for some, even held in the hand.

The place, wherever we choose, is gonnae emerge roond a corner and it will be strange and familiar. We've probably been past before, looked in the empty windows, gone, 'I hope they're doin alright for themselves'; gone, 'I hope they make it through.' But it will be there and it will be open and some a us will meet ootside, by chance. It'll be clumsy, like a first date. Do ye go in for the hug? Is that even allowed yet? Do ye say the unsaid? We'll get past all that though, all that fuss, 'cause there's a path laid oot for us, one we remember well.

Here's how it'll be. There will be soft light; in a perfect

world, it's aboot half-three, four in the pm. There will be just enough folk in; the place isnae rammed, but no dead either. There will be a table empty at the back, wi enough seats for awbody. No one will hover; no one will havetae ask, 'This seat taken, pal?' Awbody will be present, awbody correct. It'll be strange at first, fair enough, but that's tae be expected; the auld ways will reveal themselves soon enough.

We will feel a rush at gettin a round in. That small joy of standin, watchin the bronze shine on the taps, what folk want runnin through yer mind. Maybe someone's drivin, maybe someone's aff it. Nae worries. Say nae mair. Ye can have a water or a juice or whatever ye fancy. Nae judgement here; no today. If ye're skint, don't sweat it either; we've got ye covered. This is a place where, for a couple a quid, ye can just be. Sit doon, settle in, and be. There's others ahead of ye in the queue; fair enough, ye've got the time. It'll feel good to say, 'On you go' to a person ye can see.

After, ye'll bring the glasses over two by two, and everyone'll go, 'Thanks pal', and ye'll go, 'Nae bother', and believe it too. 'Cause it's only cash; it means nothin at all right now. Later on, the system is gonnae fall apart and awbody will end up deep in debt to awbody else. Folk'll spend crazy money and do it happily; they're buyin somethin mair than the thing they're buyin. Money is a token traded gladly for small pleasures: this light, this table, these walls, and the words spoke within.

'Cause we'll want tae speak. We'll want tae hear the new stories fresh; we'll want the greatest hits on repeat too. We want the laughs, when they come, tae get us by surprise, by force. We want tae be creased over, shakin heids, our beaks in the head of whatever we're drinkin. We want there tae be this big main chat goin on, but we need the mini ones too. The wee extras on the side. This pair couldnae care less aboot politics, so they've started somethin in the corner aboot somethin on the telly, somethin they've read. We want tae be on the side a somethin, and hear this one mad line an turn an be like, 'Eh? What was that?' We want folk to vanish for what seems like hours, then reappear, an it turns oot we were just distractit, busy wi whatever else. We want time no tae matter; last orders is this horizon we hope to skirt.

For a while, we might seek distraction; fae those we've lost, fae the things taken aff us. But they'll be here, the missin. Just oot a focus, fuzzed in the stained-glass, they'll be gathered roond tae feel part of it, part a somethin precious an temporary. An maybe one a us does greet and maybe one a us does get pissed off; so what. Bring what ye carry to this table and let it rest. As we work, these weights will be portioned up, divided, shared; bet ye any money ye'll leave wi less than ye brought. An honestly too: somethin sincere, spoke wi conviction an pain, an, for this night, lackin irony or sarcasm; that will gain oor respect forever.

But here's the promise: we will be thegether, wi nothin inbetween, no space or time; just this drink, an perhaps another, an we will say cheers to each other, an this cheers will be given for the cheers itsel, for the true gift of sayin it aloud, for reachin clumsily to catch those you've missed, for the bell sound of real glass touchin real glass, ringin clear throughout whatever place this is.

'To the good times,' we will say. 'Always.'

Celebrating Is as Easy as ABC
Alison Coyle

Abandon all cares and
Blast out favourite songs.
Consume certain caterpillar cakes.
Dance until your feet burn.
Eat it all!
Fly that flag.
Give grateful thanks.
Hug, hug, hug.
Indulge in ice cream.
Jump in a puddle.
Kick up your heels.
Laugh!
Make a joyful noise.
Nearly forgot the gin!
Open the curtains and let the light in.
Prosecco, piñatas, pass the parcel.
Quiet contemplation.
Ring out those bells.
Sing!
Treat yourself with kindness.
Uplift, upward, up, uP, UP!
Viva la vida!
Wine, dine, everything fine.
X-rated dance moves.
YOLO – so enjoy
Zoomies around the garden (if you're a spaniel).

Aisig dhomh gàirdeachas do shlàinte

Eòghan Stiùbhart

Aisig dhomh gàirdeachas do shlàinte

ro-ràdh

tha còrr is fichead facal ann
 airson am faireachdainn seo a labhairt
tha còrr is fichead facal ann
 airson am modh seo a chur am brìgh
tha còrr is fichead facal ann
 airson an ciall seo a chur an cèill
tha còrr is fichead facal ann
 airson an luathghair a thuigsinn
tha còrr is fichead facal ann
 airson an cùram a chur air chùl
tha còrr is fichead facal ann
 airson an gaol seo a thoirt gu buil

aoibhneas ro-aoibhneas mòr-aoibhneas
aobhachd aighear àgh
rosgal eadhann sogan sògh
meanmna meadhail meoghail mùirn
sodan sunnd subhachas sòlas
boch is beadarachd
greadhnachas is gean
toileachas is tlachd
aiteas is èibhneas is gàirdeachas
's ann às gach facal ud bheir sinn sonas
's nì sinn e gach àite
aisig dhomh gàirdeachas do shlàinte

Cuin a chaidh nàdar na ghàire airson a' chiad uair?
Cuin bho thùs a thug màthair
sòlas às an t-saoghal ùr sin
ri shuain na h-uchd?
a dh'aindeoin no air sgàth a' chràidh na cruachan
an fhalamhachd ùr na broinn mar thràigh thraoighte
gu luath fo làn mòr buan a' ghràidh aoibhnich
ri a cladaichean an còmhnaidh
an sàl an impis cur thairis
ach gun a cur fodha fhathast

san uamh sin ann an Afraga, ma 's e Eubha no ainm eile
a bh' oirre
no air cliathaich an rathaid à Srath Nabhair no ann an
lùchairtean nan uachdaran salach
mheal gach tè a h-àl, bu gheal dhi a h-iseanan
a mac strodhail air na meangannan àrda, a nighean
ealamh a' ruith na gaoithe
agus nuair a thog iad an sgiathan, chunnaic i iad a'
cuibhleadh air falbh
thar na fàire 's ged a bha a' mhuir fhathast làn, cha robh
fuaim ann ach na tuinn
ach air madainn òg, 's a' ghrian ag èirigh os cionn nam
beanntan ri cùl
dèanar leatha gàirdeachas oir bidh iad ag èirigh air
sgiathan àlainn ùr
a' tilleadh dhan nead, dhan ghèig, dhan lic,
dhan òiteag bhlàth a chùmas i air sgèith
's a' freagairt a tagraidh dhan ghaoith
aisig dhomh gàirdeachas do shlàinte

tha drùchd-gean air mo ghruaidh
boinneagan de dhealt an t-slèibh
mac na braiche, sùgh an eòrna
's comanachadh againn a-nochd
gun aran ach le ar leòr de dh'fhìon dearg
pàilteas leann is Teann a-nall
gliongadaich binn nan glainneachan dùrachdach
siud an t-slàinte chùramach
òlamaid gu sunndach i
fallas air ar malaidhean a' dannsa air ùrlar dèile
Mac an t-Saoir is Mac a' Ghobhainn
a' locradh 's a' bualadh phùirt air feadh an taighe
an teallach dearg-theth le teine ar beadarachd
's anail aighearach ar càirdeas

's èiridh mi gu socair 's canaidh mi gu solt
oidhche mhath dhuibh 's leibh uile sonas

's an ath mhadainn
an càirdeas sin a bheir oirnn èirigh 's iomain
's èirigh 's iomain 's èirigh
gus an ruig sinn na binnein
a' fàgail ar cinn ghoirt agus ar n-aithreachas
mu làr a' ghlinne trì mìle troigh fodhainn
mar na sgòthan gan ais-thionndadh
's tusa a' togail fhèineagan 's sinne an uchd a chèile
mo bheannachd ort 's m' anail nad chuideachd
do ghàire a' sìneadh mar gach cuan bhuam
's do chàirdeas cho saillte ach cho ùr
gam ath-nuadhachadh le sluaisreadh do shùgraidh
aisig dhomh gàirdeachas do shlàinte

nuair a ghabh mi mo chiad cheumannan
aig na cèilidhean is discos dheugairean
ann an tallaichean tiona na h-Àirde
comharran badminton 's crogain bhlàth
's na gillean na bu ghlice a-muigh
air an starsaich leis a' cheò 's a' chòmhradh
cha tàinig samhla dhomh
air a' ghàirdeachas a dhèanainn
còig bliadhna ri teachd
nuair a shuidheadh tu rim thaobh
air staidhre an aonaidh
a' creidsinn gur bu mhi cuideigin eile
- bha thu ceart le sin ma dh'fhaoidte
glèidhidh mi làithean d' fhèilltean fhathast
gach ceann-là rùnach na mo chridhe
nuair a bhios abhainn mo thoinisg na dìle-bhathte
's an steall a' seirm le dàil nan linn

fèis no feis
srac no sràc
tha na comharran beaga
gar roinn o chàch
ach chan fhaighear
fear seach fear
no tè seach tè
as aonais na h-eile
mar gum faighte
gaol gun mhiann
no buille gun phian

aisig dhomh gàirdeachas do shlàinte

far nach eil taisbeanadh thèid an sluagh a dhìth
's gu dearbh aig na h-òrdughan,
cha d' rinn e sùgradh no mire
ach gun teagamh 's e comharrachadh a bh' ann
le aoibhneas 's aotromachd eile
's a' leughadh san cheathramh rann thairis air fichead
aig an ochdamh salm deug thairis air còig fichead
lean a shùilean na faclan 's ghluais a bheul

is seo an là a rinn an Tighearna;
dèanaibh gàirdeachas
agus bitheamaid ait air

an uairsin mar fhreagairt air an taisbeanadh
chaidh brìgh nam faclan ud
a chur an cèill san ioma-fhuaimneachd
tro mheadarachd a rinneadh do Sheanad Earra-
ghaidheil
le Leathanach, Stiùbhartach 's Caimbeulach
fad air falbh o fhàsach tioram 's muir Ghalilee

seo fhèin an là a dh'ordaich Dia sam bi sinn suilbhir ait

as dèidh an t-searmoin 's a' bheannachaidh
air latha gaothach Siarach
choisich e às an eaglais
a' falbh leis fhèin dhachaigh
's bha i fhèin ga fhèitheamh thall
san ùir ri taobh a' chladaich
's bha aoibhneas na dheòir
an aoibhneas san ath-aithris
an aoibhneas sin a tha dlùth do bhròn

an nasg a neartaicheas
a cheanglas sinn nar cràdh
an aoibhneas a bhios cuide rinn

aisig dhomh gàirdeachas do shlàinte

coda

is milse gàirdeachas d' fhaclan na mo chluais
is ò nach àghmhor am bruadar a thig gu bith
an tlachd is an toileachas na do chuideachd
an iarmailt shoilleir, a' toirt deagh ghean
leanabhan an àigh, sonas nan seanpharantan
's lachan na tè àlainn a' dannsa gu dlùth
's greadhnachas geal driùchd na maidne
far an lùiginn fhèin a bhith a ghnàth
aisig dhomh gàirdeachas do shlàinte

Restore to me the joy of your salvation – a translation of sorts

There is simply no single Gaelic word for celebration – there are dozens – either expressing a form of great joy or words for occasions and events marking either the sacred or the profane, and sometimes both at once.

prelude

there are more than twenty words
      to speak this feeling
      to give essence to this mood
      to express this meaning
      to understand the exultation
      to put all care behind
      to bring this love to bear

joy

great joy

deep joy

joy joy joy
      joy joy joy joy
            joy joy joy joy
joy joy joy joy
      joy and joy
            joy and joy
                 joy and joy
                 joy and joy and joy
from every word we take that joy
and enact it everywhere

1 - mother

when did instinct first become a smile?
when did the first mother rejoice at the new life asleep at
her breast?
despite or because of the agony of her hips

the new emptiness within her like an exposed beach
swiftly submerged under the eternal high tide of joyful
love
always at her shores
the brine always threatening to spill over
but never yet inundating her

in that African cave, if she was named Eve or something
else
or on the road from Strathnaver, or in the palaces of the
filthy rich
each one enjoyed her brood, her mother's pride, her
little birds

her prodigal son on the highest boughs, her swift
daughter chasing the wind
and when they raised their wings, she saw them wheel
away
over the horizon, and only the tide remained, there was
no sound but the waves
but in the young morning, the sun rising over the
mountains to her back
she celebrates because they are rising on new beautiful
wings
returning to nest and ledge and branch
to the warm thermals that keep her flying
and answering her petition to the wind

restore to me the joy of your salvation

2 – sons and daughters of the malt

I have tears of joy on my cheeks
droplets of the mountain dew
the son of the malt, the cream of the barley
as we hold a communion tonight
with no bread but enough vino rosso
plenty of ale and Teann a-nall
the sweet clinking of the welcoming glasses
siud an t-slàinte chùramach
òlamaid gu sunndach i
fallas air ar malaidhean a' dannsa air ùrlar dèile
MacIntyre and Smith
planing and hammering tunes throughout the hostelry
the forge red-hot with the fire of our celebration
and the joyful breath of our friendship

and I will gently rise and I'll softly call
good night and joy be with you all

and the next morning
this friendship makes us rise and drive
and rise and drive and rise
until we reach the peaks
leaving our sore heads and shame
on the valley floor three thousand feet below
like the clouds inverted
you take selfies as we squeeze in close
my blessing on you as I breathe easy in your company
your smile stretches like all the oceans before me
and your friendship so salty yet so fresh
renewing me with the lapping waves of your joking

restore to me the joy of your salvation

3 - sweetheart

when I took those first steps
at the ceilidhs and teenage discos
in the tin huts of the Aird
marked for badminton and drinking warm cans
whilst the smarter lads were outside
on the steps with the smoke and the chat
I had no inkling
of the celebration that I would hold
five years later
when you'd sit next to me
on the union steps
thinking I was someone else
– perhaps you were right about that

I keep your feast days still
each secret anniversary of my heart
when the full river of my feelings overflows
and the deluge sings with the tryst of ages

festival or sex*
a tear or a stroke
it's the little marks
that separate us from each other
but we can't get
one or the other
one or the other
without the other one
as if you could get
love without desire
a punch without pain

restore to me the joy of your salvation

*the difference between fèis – festival – and feis – sex – is
a grave accent. The Gaelic for a grave accent is sràc,
which can also mean a stroke or a blow; without the
accent srac means tear or rip*

4 – father

Where there is no vision the people perish

indeed at the communions
he did not have any jollity or play
but it was without doubt a form of celebration
with joy and lightness of another sort
and reading the 24th verse
of the 118th psalm
his eyes followed the words and he mouthed

*this is the day that the Lord has made
we shall rejoice
and be glad in it*

then as if in response to the vision
the essence of those words
was expressed in heterophony
through a meter devised for the Argyll Synod
by McLaine, Stewart and Campbell
far away from the desert land and the Sea of Galilee

*this is the day that the Lord has made, we shall rejoice
and be glad in it*

after the sermon and the benediction
on a windy Westside day
he walked from the church

alone home
and she was waiting for him
in the soil by the shore
and there was joy in his tears
the joy in repetition
the joy that is so close to sorrow
the bond that strengthens
and connects us in our pain
the joy that stays with us

restore to me the joy of your salvation

coda

sweetest the rejoicing of your words in my ear
the joy in a dream that comes true
the joy and pleasure of your company
the blue sky that brings good will
the children of joy, the happiness of grandparents
the laughter of a beautiful woman dancing close
and the bright joy of the morning dew
in the place where I long to be always

restore to me the joy of your salvation

Hello, Hello, Hello!
What do we have here, Sir?

Mary Topp

Julie wanted me to wear blue. A long, slim empire-line dress of sea-blue lace with a pale turquoise lining was made for me. I was fifteen years old, wore specs and could not really believe that the eldest sibling of my special friend had chosen me to be her bridesmaid, or that I would be wearing such a beautiful dress. I'd known the family since we moved next door when I was four years old. I had often shouted to her mum from a tree in their garden.

'Mrs Dee-ee. I'm stuck.'

I think Julie had come to help me down once, too. I was a bit of a tomboy and a nuisance! She had two younger brothers, the youngest being my age and my best chum, with whom I shared many adventures. Julie left home first, to become a nurse. Now she was back before marrying her Scottish doctor, Angus.

On the day, I waited outside the local village church for Julie and her father. My parents were ushered inside with all the other guests by Julie's brothers. Angus and his best man loitered before the altar. Mrs D sat in the front pew dressed in a pale lemon coat-dress with matching cloche hat. The organ played softly. Just as the village clock struck twice, the car arrived and Julie was helped out by her father. I'd never seen Mr D without his cravat, but somehow he maintained the air of a French teacher even in a morning suit, that most English of attire. She looked lovely in a snug-fitted ivory silk dress with three-quarter-length lace sleeves. The scooped neckline had a lace modesty panel and she wore her veil over her face. They walked up to the great oak door of the church between the pine trees and tombstones as the photographer took the first of many photos. I fell in behind as she entered the porch and the organist switched to Handel's 'Wedding March'. Many heads turned to watch us process down the aisle and finally Angus too looked round, smiling as she joined him. They went forward to stand in front of the vicar, who stood beside a large arrangement of lilies, yellow roses and agapanthus. The sun shone through the stained-glass windows above the altar and the church felt warm as the vicar welcomed us.

I had learnt the words to the first hymn, 'Love Divine, All Loves Excelling', at school, so joined in lustily. We listened to the three causes for which matrimony was ordained. I was glad to see no one stepped forward to admit an impediment to their union. Then Julie turned to give me her flowers and the best man passed the ring to the vicar for the exchange of vows. Angus's soft Scottish accent announced,

'I, Angus Donald, take thee, Julie Anne, to be my wedded wife, to have and to hold from this day forward, for better or for...'

The rest was drowned in an almighty crash as the vicar collapsed into the flowers. The stunned silence was quickly followed by a collective gasp from the congregation. Nurse Julie and Doctor Angus looked at one another but stayed perfectly still and I took my stance from them. There was movement behind us and two friends, presumably doctors, stepped up to help the vicar onto his feet and bundle him out of the church. The best man recovered the ring and the bible and reinstated the flower arrangement as best he could.

So what now? A pause ensued and then came the realisation that Angus and Julie had miraculously also catered for this eventuality. Another friend, a rector, appeared and continued the service. I made a mental note to ensure a doctor and a rector were invited to my wedding should I ever find a special someone. We sang the final hymn, 'Praise, My Soul, the King of Heaven', with fervour and giving extra thanks before returning up the aisle towards the sunlight. Julie and Angus stood outside to welcome their guests, many of whom I did not know.

A little bored now the service was over, I was gazing into the distance when the sun glinted on the gold stitches of a brocade cloth. The stole was lying on one of the tombs. I stepped back to get a better view through the pines and could see the local bobby was interviewing the two doctors who had helped the vicar. The reverend was sitting on a tombstone looking somewhat dishevelled. What was going on? Surely the medics were not going to be arrested?

Later that week, in the local newspaper, we read the headline,

'Two men strip vicar on tombstone outside village church.'

Underneath, the story was slightly less sensational and started:

'A member of the Cheshire Constabulary investigated an incident outside Goostrey Parish Church. The policeman had seen two men stripping the vicar while he lay comatose on a tombstone. A victim of our recent hot weather, the Reverend Park had succumbed to the heat in church when conducting a wedding. On closer inspection the two doctors, who were present in the congregation, were found to be loosening his upper garments to allow him to breathe more freely and so aid his recovery.'

Author note: *I attended the Golden Anniversary celebrations of Julie and Angus last year and we all laughed about that day 50 years ago when they were married. I have changed names but not the place. I am not a published author of fiction but in my previous job as a curator at NMS Edinburgh, now retired, I wrote catalogues.*

Share your love of books. . .

Scottish Book Trust is an independent national charity. Our mission is to ensure people living in Scotland have equal access to books.

If you're enjoying this book, please consider making a donation so that everyone in Scotland has the opportunity to improve their life chances through books and the fundamental skills of reading and writing.

Visit **scottishbooktrust.com/support** to find out more.

Family treasures

Mon the Rovers
Alan Gillespie

Stark's Park wisnay big enough so we hud tae go tae
Edinburra. Easter Road, where Hibs played. I just mind
there being hunners ay green seats. I says tae my da,
how could they no huv played in Kirkcoddy? He says,
cos there's no enough seats. This is Bah-yerr Myoonick
we're talking about, ken. This is Kahn. Papin. Klinsmann.

Big wow, I thought. We'd already pumped they
Faroeeze dumplings, Gøtu Ítróttarfelag. Took ages tae
learn how tae pronounce that name, and I never forgot
it. In the next round we stuffed some mob frae Iceland
called Akraness, and both they games got played at
Stark's Park. So I didnay see what was so special about
the Germans. Wisnay as if they were gonnay bring a
million folk over for the game, eh?

We got the supporters' bus frae Kirkcoddy tae
Edinburra and there wis a few boys frae my school on it.
I mind everybody being dead relaxed. Cos, like, we were
undefeated in Europe, ken. Somebody said, whit tae dae
is hold them aff until half-time. That'll get them nervous
and we'll turn them over in the second half. Easy. Then
the grown-ups did a sweepstake and it wis like, aye,
Rovers, wan-nil, nae bother.

That wis some Rovers team, though. Scott Thomson
in goals; the same Scott Thomson that saved the penalty
frae Paul McStay and won us the Coca-Cola Cup. So he wis
basically like Superman and it wis a total mystery why they
two plonkers Leighton and Goram were getting intay the
Scotland team ahead ay him. Davie Sinclair wis at centre-

back, and he wis the hardest man in fitba. Hud tattoos on his teeth, apparently. Him and big Shaun Dennis were a couplay mentalcases, nae doubt. In midfield ye had the two wee diamonds, Micky Cameron and Danny Lennon. As good as anybody on their day. There was the Trinidadian on the bench, Tony Rougier, and he wis mibbe my favourite, an aw-dancin', aw-singin', out-and-out winger. If ye ask me, he should've started the match. But it wouldnay do tae question the manager, Sir Jimmy Nicholl. Ye just didnay question that man's decisions.

I sat with my da behind Scott Thomson's goal. A teacher frae my school wis a few rows behind us. I waved and he waved back and it wis like we werenay teacher and pupil anymore. We were Rovers. Two Rovers.

I mind looking across the pitch tae the other stand, which wis fullay Rovers fans too. Someone'd made a giant banner that says, ROVERS GET MUNICH, PARS GET GREENOCK. The Pars hud just been relegated tae the first division, and Raith were league cup holders, Premier League, holding our ain with the best in Europe. I points it out tae my da. Aye, he says, that's a good banner.

Klinsmann scored in, like, six seconds. The ball bounced just outside the box, Scott Thomson comes charging out, and gets lobbed. We're aw silent afore the ball even touches the net. The whole stadium, the whole ay Edinburra, silent. Then someone goes, mon the Rovers. And someone else goes, aye, mon the Rovers. Then everyone, everyone, me, my da, my teachers, the boys frae school, we're up and we're all going, MON THE ROVERS! MON THE ROOOVEEERS!

Ye might no believe it if ye werenae there, but for the next half-hour we battered them. Cameron and Lennon were wee schemers in midfield, big Ally Graham up front wis getting his heid tae everything, and mad Davie

Sinclair wis bombing forward frae the back. I mind the German goalie, Kahn, trying tae waste time so Sinky picks him up and chucks him intay the advertising boards.

Jimmy Nicholl finally listened tae me and brought on Rougier in the second half. With his first touch he nutmegged Ziege and went skipping up the wing, twinkly-toed, heid down. We battered them. Could've scored. Should've scored.

Klinsmann's second goal seemed tae come frae nowhere. Papin wis oan and went on a mazy and pit it in the box and next thing ye know the net's bulging and the place is silent again. Klinsmann's blond heid's racing away tae the half-dozen German fans in the corner. I looked at my da and he shook his head and he didnae have tae tell me, it wis over.

We sang Geordie Munro aw the way hame frae Edinburra. When we got back tae my da's flat he stuck the news oan and made us cheese on toast. It wis the English news. They says it's been a good night for British teams in Europe. Scot Gemmill's goal won the game for Nottingham Forest in their tie. And Raith Rovers failed to upset the odds against the German giants, Bayern Munich, who won thanks to two Jurgen Klinsmann goals. And now, the weather.

Everybody kens whit happened in the second leg. Danny Lennon scores a free kick and the Rovers are winning by a goal at half-time before the Germans come back. But I'll always mind the first leg best. That night in Edinburra with my da.

Author note: *My dad took me to the first leg when Raith Rovers played Bayern Munich in the UEFA Cup. We got beat, but played them off the park.*

Mum's Shoes: A Celebration
Britta Benson

Please note: this piece contains descriptions some readers may find upsetting.

I've heard about women who hide new shoes from their husbands. A friend of mine calls this behaviour her 'one little flaw'. She shows off expensive designer products, bought by the uncontrollable desire of a whim. Pretty, impractical fashion choices, often regretted as soon as unwrapped back home and then kept out of sight in their box.

My story is not about flashy new shoes, but a celebration of something old, bashed and borrowed. It's about the size of feet, the extent of a life and why it's so easy to love generous imperfection. It's also about hallway cupboards. Take mine, for example.

There, in the deepest, darkest corner, behind the walking boots, the formal shoes, my wellingtons, even further back than my suspiciously crisp-looking running shoes, sits a pair of soft brown suede shoes that are not mine, hiding ever so discreetly and without the slightest complaint. They don't make a fuss, but as soon as I open the cupboard, I can smell them. Not in a bad way, there's just that whiff of suede shoe cleaner, the faintest of perfumes.

The story of this pair of brown suede shoes begins many years ago. I don't know when they were bought. I only know that in July 2018, when I sat with my mum in her garden on a nice sunny day, she was wearing those shoes and they looked completely unremarkable. Slightly old and done.

'They'll see me out,' Mum said, and she was adamant. She would not buy any more new shoes. 'It would be such a waste of money, pet.'

'I'll order you a new pair,' I replied. All of Mum's shoes came from the comfort shoe mail order catalogue. The same model, over and over again, the only type she ever liked. No-fuss lace-ups, built to last.

'I'd never get the mileage out of a new pair.'

'Those shoes have clearly seen better days, Mum.'

'So have I, dear,' Mum replied, 'so have I. They stay and that's that. I'll not walk very far any more. I'm dying. They will do me just fine.'

I waited for her to say 'only joking', but she meant it. And as always, she was right.

Those brown suede shoes faithfully walked Mum's last miles with her, mainly to the taxi driving her to the hospital and back. They got her to chemotherapy appointments and to her letterbox to get the newspaper. Sometimes they even got her to the shops. Not the big supermarket in the other village, just down to the corner shop at the end of our street. The miles quickly became yards and the yards turned into token gestures, slow, muffled shuffles, supported by a Zimmer frame until suddenly, the brown suede shoes were put in the cupboard in her hallway, where they stayed put for a while, even when Mum's body was taken away in September 2019. She didn't need her shoes for that last journey.

When she died, I started to cling to the objects that had belonged to her. I stroked the facecloth I had wiped her forehead with during those endless final days and nights, listening to a breath that threatened to stop any moment. I clutched her handbag, jam-packed with the 'just in case' items. She'd spent more than 70 years being prepared for every eventuality: broken fingernails, blisters on feet, snotty children and grandchildren, assorted throat sweeties from years long past, a sewing kit, pins, paper clips, pens and notepads.

And then there were her shoes. I took them out of the cupboard again and put them on my feet. We share the same shoe size and I walked in Mum's shoes in the days after her death. It was the only way I could move forward, or move at all, to be honest. It was a start. The beginning of the rest of my life in new old shoes. I was literally moving on.

Now, I take them out every now and again. Not very often, but on special days. Some people celebrate family occasions with cake. I wear Mum's last pair of shoes to go to places she liked. For her 77th birthday celebration, I took her brown suede shoes to the seaside and got them covered in the wet, salty sand of the beach in Troon. We were there as a family before she got ill. It brought me closer to that one beautiful moment, when all was well. I went to the hospital in Mum's shoes to celebrate the arrival of our new grandchild, thus making sure she was there, when this latest addition to the family was welcomed by all. On the anniversary of her death I took a walk in her shoes down the canal, again full of memories of shared joyful days, shared lives. Even in the robust autumn breeze I could still smell the suede care and protection spray. They have been impregnated for eternity, not even the Scottish rain can penetrate them.

Mum's in my heart, of course, but from time to time it feels good to walk in her shoes as a very private celebration of the person she was. No nonsense, but soft and unfortunately breaking.

One day, I know, I'll have to let go of them. They looked slightly sad in the summer of 2018 and they are clearly nearing the end of their journey. Those shoes have done far more miles than they were ever expected to. When the day comes, I'll be ready. Until then, I enjoy the company of this secret pair. My sneaky reminder, my personal ritual and a very private celebration. My husband knows about the shoes, by the way, and he even says 'hi' to them, whenever I dig them out. They have personality. What can I say? My mum left her trace, her footprint, in my life, my heart and my family.

Author note: *When I read that the competition was about celebration, I instantly thought of the way I celebrate my mum's life and include her in the major celebrations happening now, after her death – through her shoes, which may seem odd but makes perfect sense to my family.*

4 Cubed
Kathryn Holme, Byre Writers

4
of us, enveloped in love and encouragement.
Our home, our refuge from stressful thoughts and unkind
actions.
My husband and I taking turns to worry, to comfort, to
praise.
Facing problems together, hand-in-hand.
Celebrating successes like my husband's first 10k run.

16
my eldest will be later this year.
A triathlete in training, avid reader, expert baker and
Eurovision fanatic.
I'm proud of him for how he has coped with National 5
assessments.
My youngest is almost 12, approaching the end of primary
school days.
An environmentalist, obsessed with Lego. Full of
fascinating facts told through his newly broken voice.
Not your typical adolescent boys.
I cherish them.

64
weeks unemployed. My status undefined. Who am I now?
Just Mum?
Empowered by my family's support, resilience shines
through.
I study online. Give myself permission to write.
Priorities now changed, I am more at peace with myself.
My own personal celebration.

Author note: *I value the support from my family and
wrote this piece for them as a thank you.*

An Ordinary Day
Marianne L Berghuis

My husband, Tony, loves driving, and we desperately needed to escape the constricted walls of our home. Tony drove the B-roads with no real destination in mind. At each junction he slowed down and asked, left or right? Mack and Peter chose eagerly from the back seats, and on we went. Apart from weekly hospital trips to Edinburgh, we'd not been anywhere for months. We'd been isolated long before Covid was even a thing. The sight of copper-brown hedgerows and stretched-out yellow fields seemed like a luxury. We stopped at a bakery to buy juice and buttered rolls to squash salt and vinegar crisps into. Tony never appreciates the delicacy and crunch of crisp butties, so he bought himself a steak bridie. Makeshift picnic in hand, we finally unfurled out of the hot car onto Elie Beach.

*

We look like any other family enjoying a bright April afternoon. Tony is walking along the shoreline. Peter is splashing in the water with his trouser-legs rolled up above his knees. We've no spare clothes or towels, I think to myself. Mack and I are sitting on outstretched jackets, staring out across the ocean. Mack's two black crutches, stick upright in the sand, like some kind of mast waiting for windsocks to be attached.

'I'm not going paddling, Mum,' Mack says.

'That's okay,' I reply.

I put both my arms around him and squeeze tight.

'I get really jealous, Mum.'

'How do you mean?' I ask.

'Seeing Petey jumping in the waves; he's so happy.'

I say nothing and watch Peter. He is getting soaked as the waves ebb in and out. Seawater splashing up, catching the bottom of his black 'Dan TDM' hoodie. Its bright diamond logo reflects the sun and casts extra shimmers upon the glittery sand. Mack is right, Peter does look happy. I haven't seen him so carefree in a long time. His dimpled smile and small, slim frame innocently jump the breaking waves at the edge of a vast ocean. I glance over towards Tony; he, too, looks brighter. His tense shoulders a little lower.

'I want to be like that again. Just like any other kid. I hate what's happened to me,' Mack says, breaking the silence.

'I know, I hate it too Mack. We have to keep going though.'

I can feel my eyes welling up. I know he finds it hard. We all do, but Mack especially. He's been through more than any 13-year-old ever should.

'I know I'm lucky, Mum, I just want more.'

I turn to face him. 'It's not bad to want your mobility back, Mack. It's what anyone would want after all that treatment.'

'My leg is gonna get stronger, Mum, I know it. My foot might stay smaller but it got a much bigger dose of Grays, remember?'

Mack looks at me knowledgeably; he has become wise beyond his years during these last 22 months.

'Grays?'

'That's the unit radiotherapy is measured in. Then the total dose is split into fractions. My foot got an extra week's blasting.' Mack asks.

'How do you know all that stuff?' I laugh. 'My head was a blur half the time.'

'I find the science stuff interesting, just wish it wasn't about me,' Mack says shrugging his shoulders.

'You're doing well with your physio though, your mobility is improving. You'll get walking with one crutch soon.'

'I hate physio,' says Mack.

'I know, you tell me every time we go! It's made such a difference though.'

'Still hate it!'

We're interrupted by shouts from Peter and Tony, who are waving at us frantically.

'It'll be a crab or something. You go, Mum, or they won't stop shouting. I'll stay here.'

'You sure?' I ask

'Yeah, it's fine, sitting I can do!'

I walk towards the others feeling tearful. After all he's been through, I can tell Mack is lonely and isolated in a way that has nothing to do with the pandemic. Peter is holding something in his hands. He proudly shows me pieces of blue-tinged pottery and matt, green sea glass. One piece is shaped like Africa. We used to collect sea glass and turn it into pretty pictures of boats or birds. That was before, when both boys could clamber freely over rocks and explore coastlines looking for shimmering treasure. Peter places his finds in Tony's large jacket pocket. Then we crouch down to look for more. A while later I look back to check on Mack. He isn't there. Panic rises through my body.

Scanning the area, I spot him on the shoreline further up the beach. Shoes off. Joggies rolled up. Mack is balancing on his crutches and standing with his feet in the water. He glances over, smiles and waves. Tony and I look at each other.

Peter instantly races off to join him.

Tony and I have tears in our eyes. Both our boys jumping the waves. Peter screeches with laughter. The weight through Mack's arms pushes his crutches deeper into the sand. He lets the water lap up over his feet. I worry the rubber bungs on the ends of the crutches will come off. Mack's smaller, radiotherapy-mottled foot is raised, sweeping back and forth in the chilly water. The splash of the waves, and Peter's enthusiasm, soak Mack.

'It's freezing, Mum!' Mack shouts.

Tony makes joyful whooping sounds. I kick my shoes off and join the boys. We jump and squeal at how cold the April sea is. The grin on Mack's face has been absent for 22 months. Today is a good day. That alone is cause for celebration.

Author note: *The first time we left the house after my son was no longer on the shielding register, we just drove. We had been isolating before Covid due to my son's treatment for cancer, so it felt extremely special to go out. His foot and restricted mobility bothered him and he was very self-conscious. This is the day when things began to really look up.*

Painted Nails
Lisa C

We have the same hands, and take a modest pride in the long fingers and elegantly shaped nails the women of our family share. You feel at your best when you have your nails painted and, every once in a while, I'll receive a photo from the care home of you in your chair, freshly permed backlit hair, long beads and rosary in position. A hand turned to the camera, pink nails shining like your smile.

Given everything you have suffered through in life, and the many hard losses you have endured, it may seem shallow to focus on the joy you find in the act of dressing up. But it doesn't feel that way to me, Gran. The way you live is a celebration of the simple pleasures, of the right you have to treat yourself, to consider yourself worthy of some shimmer, some style.

Those photos send a beautiful statement about your resilience and your unwillingness to give up the personal habits that make you who you are. They are reminders that you are a woman who, despite current limitations, will express herself as she pleases, for her own pleasure. A woman who can take a few minutes to do something kind for herself.

You loved when my sister and I used to come to your flat with our shopping bags, showing off whatever daft new sequined top or backless dress we had bought in town.

You celebrated us through our messy teenage years as we figured out who we wanted to be, who we wanted to be with, how we wanted to live. We must have looked a state at times, with poorly dyed hair and dodgy makeup, but you never let on. Partnering up, breaking down, going out with friends and staying in to study – you soaked it all in and spurred us on.

When you were young you didn't have those chances to be flawed, free and changeable. You worked, you married, you raised your family, you kept your house, and you turned your attentions everywhere but on yourself.

It is easy to imagine feeling bitter, seeing how young women live now. To grudge the opportunities you missed, and to wonder what might have been. Instead, you loved to see all the frivolous and carefree parts of our lives, laughing as we shared our missteps, running your hands over our purchases approvingly, making them feel special to us.

We have not sat beside you in that way for over a year now. You have been in quarantine, have suffered with Covid, have had many falls, and you have been moved to a new care home without a choice in the matter. Your speech has worsened and your ability to read the books and magazines you love has lessened. We do not know how much you understand about the world outside the care home from one day to the next. And that is why these little expressions of selfhood and autonomy mean so much more than they would otherwise. They are a declaration that you will not surrender your joy in the face of the world's cruelties.

And when I look at my hands, my fingertips, and compare them to those photos of your own, I am reminded of everything you have given me and everything we must celebrate when we see each other again. Your spirited embrace of the fun and the glamour in life has taught me a valuable lesson. By showing us the example of a woman with poise and dignity, a woman worth celebrating, you make it so much easier to believe the same about ourselves.

Author note: *This piece was inspired by a photo of my gran, Margaret Erskine, which I received from staff at her care home during the pandemic. Those little attempts to connect and share positive updates meant so much to my family during the pandemic.*

A Life Well Lived
Julie Drybrough

*Please note: this piece contains descriptions some
readers may find upsetting.*

It's hard to find the celebration in an unexpected death.

When an ending is sudden and unforeseen, you are
caught wholly unprepared. One day things are this way:
life is moving, plans are in place, this person is there, the
future has a course. Then in moments, seconds, hours,
the whole shape of everything shifts so fast. You are left,
staring at holes that cannot be patched. Squinting into a
bright light of realisation: nothing will ever be as it was.

Our dad died, unexpectedly, on a random Wednesday
in September. Four days before he and I were due to
meet for lunch. The day before his car tax was due.
On the day of his penultimate Church Choral Society
practice. He left behind his wife, three children, three
grandchildren, a sister, nieces, nephews, in-laws, friends,
a middle-aged, well-behaved black lab. . .

There was no easing over the Rubicon. He was
there, and then he was not. He sat down to his usual
mid-morning *Courier* and mug of coffee. Then he was
simply. . . not alive any more. It was shocking. World-
ending.

In death, there is 'Stuff Folk Say'. Neat phrases of
condolence, commiseration, or comfort. Convention
dictates acknowledgement, so folk have to say
SOMETHING. We were generously offered well-worn
words over the phone or cups of tea; or sometimes

awkward words, from those who just-don't-quite-know-what-to-say. 'So sorry for your loss.' 'What a shock.' 'Such a lovely man.'

But neat phrases and well-worn words were so unlike Dad. We lost him, somehow, in all the niceties.

It was comforting, then, that when it came to his eulogy, we began to remember him as he was. Not polite and neat and mourned and dead, but joyful and messy and true and alive. We remembered:

The rapture that good classical music brought him.

His appreciation of a decent malt.

His cheese addiction.

His pride in us (often underlined in the groaningly awful Annual Christmas Card Letter, where our every achievement got bragging rights).

His absolute inability to tell a short story (SO much context and backstory before you got anywhere near the point).

His godawful handwriting (making shopping lists and the diaries he wrote completely impenetrable).

His habit of saying 'Aye. Right then', indicating he was about to change the subject or get up to go somewhere.

His open facial expressions – joy, disapproval, concentration – he'd have been a bloody awful poker player.

His advice: 'Dinnae be so hashy-bashy' if you were attacking something with great gusto or hazarding potential injury.

His ex-rally-driver need for speed whenever he hit a motorway.

The terrible, tuneless whistling that erupted from the garage when he was fixing something.

The never-ending car-fixing projects: Morris Minor, Beetle, the canary yellow Mark 1 Golf GTI…

How you could never leave without your car being hoovered and washed.

His insanely bushy eyebrows; one pointing up, the other down.

How he chewed his tongue when he concentrated.

His deep knowledge of the land and the soil and the seasons, meaning a running commentary on the state of crops or the ploughing decisions of a farmer when you drove anywhere with him.

His canine-magnet status: all dogs doted on him.

In remembering him, we reclaimed him, celebrated him. The pain of his death became softened as we revisited his life; well-lived and generously shared. Beyond the soft, well-worn words of sorrow, lay the sharper, funnier, more Dad-shaped stories… and it was here we found him and celebrated him again.

The hundred small things, wonderful and annoying and imperfect and beloved and wise, that made up the man. The realisation that those hundred small things became embedded in us and his grandchildren. The legacy of love he bestowed.

Because of him, his children all have a working knowledge of engines. We are practical; able to fix bike punctures, paint walls, or (less practically) shoot a clay pigeon in a freezing wind. We have inherited an inability to skip a cheese board, a taste for whisky and a rambling storytelling style. In us, is an intergenerational characteristic of being fearless in the world and believing that being polite to waitresses shows the mark of good manners and a good person. That's how we were raised, that's how we raise ours.

That's a legacy to celebrate.

Author note: *In the depths of lockdown, I heard Dermot O'Leary on the radio, asking for the awful habits and terrible things we love about the people we've lost. Some of the stories cracked me up. I remembered sitting with my brothers, in the aftermath of our father dying, and doing something similar. The conversation was so infused with love and horror – 'Do you remember how he…?' and 'That time he…?' – it felt like he could be sitting at the table, protesting and bickering with us. It felt really good.*

Share your love of books. . .

Scottish Book Trust is an independent national charity. Our mission is to ensure people living in Scotland have equal access to books.

If you're enjoying this book, please consider making a donation so that everyone in Scotland has the opportunity to improve their life chances through books and the fundamental skills of reading and writing.

Visit **scottishbooktrust.com/support** to find out more.

Quiet victories

How I Celebrate
Edinburgh Syrian Women's Group

They are more like quiet flowers, really,
my celebrations now. They unfurl softly –
more like small gifts of gentleness
than huge horse-heart triumphs.

I don't want to come in first. I want
to reach the end of a day without tears,
to see my friends again and hug them,
to feel depression lift like tiredness
after a nap. This is how I celebrate,
these days: a slow smile for each coffee
finished, each hope nourished, each small
joy.

Another Step Along the Road
Kirsty Hammond

The gates weren't locked. They never are, not for as long as I can remember. The only restriction is the sign on the entrance warning that dogs must be leashed. For most locals, the country estate is a place for exercise, to witness the passing of the seasons with snowdrops, daffodils, bluebells. To see the pigs that moved in a while back, or admire the view across the valley.

But for me, it was something else. Not a place of enjoyment, but a reminder of what had been taken from me over the past few years. That day, it was something I was determined to reclaim.

I have anxiety. It started out small, easily ignored. A few worried thoughts here, some sleepless nights there. Saying no to things I'd usually say yes to.

Then it progressed. By the time I got help, I was struggling to leave the house. The belief that something bad was going to happen became a constant companion.

Anxiety isn't logical and can be triggered by anything. A quick trip around Tesco became a mammoth task, with days of planning and mental preparation. Some people reading this won't fully understand what I'm saying. Others will appreciate it all too well.

One of the things I stopped being able to do was go for walks. The great outdoors is good for your mental health, but not when you panic just leaving your front door.

Needless to say, I got therapy (thank you, NHS). It's been a long and, at times, painful recovery, one which is still ongoing, but I eventually felt able to start doing the things I used to enjoy, albeit in baby steps. That meant five-minute walks, increasing to ten, then fifteen.

Finally, I was ready to take the next step on the road to recovery and try an hour. When I walked shorter distances, I chose routes that gave easy options to get home, but I wanted to push myself. Walking around the country estate would take an hour, with no escape route.

My heartbeat thundered in my ears as I stepped through those gates, only ten minutes into the walk. My palms were sweaty and there was a weight on my chest. All to be expected. I repeated my usual statement to myself – It might be difficult but I can do this. Step by step.

I kept going, trying not to think about how far I had to go. I split the route into small chunks in my mind, so I just had to get to the pig enclosure, five minutes away.

No pigs could be seen that day. My heart still thudded. Another reminder to myself – it's okay that it's hard, you can do this.

Next was the Big Tree, only slightly taller than the rest, in another ten minutes. I couldn't think past that.

The tree appeared. I was doing it, I was actually doing it! My next marker was the small path to the left, halfway through the route.

But my heart rate was picking up. That damn anxiety, not a voice but a certainty that I couldn't do it. It became difficult to think straight. I was starting to panic.

I squeezed my hands into fists, tight as I could, for a count of ten, then released for ten. Kept breathing. In and out. There was no danger, it was just my anxiety making me think there was.

It might be difficult, but I can do this. Step by step.

The path appeared. The point of no return, exactly halfway. I was okay, I was going to make it.

I took the path. It's the steepest section. As well as robbing me of the things I enjoy, anxiety had also taken much of my physical health. It prevented me from exercising enough, if at all. A few years ago, I would hardly be sweating on a walk like this. Now, I was panting.

Near the top of the path, there's a waterfall. It's pretty small, but when I saw it that day I thought it was one of the most beautiful things I'd ever seen. My heart was still hammering, but from exertion more than anything. Everything was sweaty, not just my hands. I no longer needed to say my statements or clench my fists. I stopped, and just breathed.

I didn't linger, unsure how long the calm would last. The rest of the route was downhill and before I knew it, I was back at the gates.

I checked the time when I got home. One hour and five minutes. The longest I'd walked in over two years. Outwardly, my celebration wasn't visible. I wrote in my exposure diary how my anxiety felt on a scale of one to ten, ready to show my therapist the following week.

Inside, I was dancing.

It had been scary. But I had done it. And if I'd done it once, I could do it again. Six months before, I hadn't been able to walk five minutes without panicking.

Anxiety is irrational. I'd done that walk hundreds of times in the past without a second thought. I'd lost so much, but I was slowly starting to reclaim it. Recovery might be a slow trek, but I was getting my life back.

There was no champagne and caviar that day. Just a cup of tea and a cheese sandwich.

But as I got tucked in, I noticed something else that had been in short supply recently. I was smiling.

And that was worth celebrating.

Author note: *Between my mental health struggles and the pandemic, I've learnt to celebrate all my wins, no matter how small. That particular day felt like a huge win and was an important step in my recovery.*

Celebration: A Definition
Abiy Orr

Because I'm autistic, celebration isn't something that comes naturally to me. In common with a lot of autistic people, I struggle to distinguish between different emotions or to have the 'right' facial expressions for what is happening around me. It's not that I don't have the same feelings, it's just that I can't define them as mainstream people do.

It's like painting, in a way. Some people get the watercolour paintboxes of life, with rows of beautiful, subtle colours: crimson lake, burnt sienna, vermilion. Others, like me, get three tubs of poster paint and are left to get on with it. Layer the watercolours over and into each other and they remain recognisable and yet modulate one another. Try that with the poster paint and you'll get the same mud brown again and again and again. That's what emotions are like for me. I can recognise happy, sad and angry, and the condition my elder boy, also autistic, describes as 'sad-and-angry', but the rest is just so much mud.

Hold on, you say: celebration isn't an emotion. It's a happening. It's a time of success, not a feeling.

Not if you're me, it isn't. If I, or people I know, win a competition or succeed at something or pass exams or get married or have a baby or find the ideal home or whatever, I feel happy. Not excited or gobsmacked or ecstatic or any other watercolour feelings, just happy. And if a group of people are happy together and celebrating, I usually find myself out of key, too unsubtle, too matt for the sparkle all around me.

Then there's the weird things mainstream people do when they're celebrating: dress up in uncomfortable clothes, eat stuff that costs a fortune and gives them indigestion, and drink alcohol until they can't remember what they were happy about in the first place and end up bickering, battering or sick. From an autistic point of view, none of this makes any sense. A lot of autistic people worry about being out of control or taken out of their comfort zone and their own routines. This is why almost none of the people in the police cells and A&E on a weekend are autistic. We're safe at home in a comfortable jumper with a good book and a nice cup of tea!

And the noise mainstreamers make when they celebrate! Yelling and squawking, clapping and stamping, banging and clattering and roaring and squealing! What in the world is that all about? A lot of autistic people don't like noise and don't like crowds: a party to a 'normal' person is an anteroom of Hades to people like me. How can you think about the thing that is making you glad when you're so busy making such a racket?

Having said all that, there was one time when I got it right. I was an odd child at school, a loner and confused, stumping around between the real teenagers, full of bewilderment and anxiety. I was bright, though, and I made it to, and through, university. I went to Aberdeen and studied at King's College, which is mostly very old and often very beautiful. Like many academic autists, I had no difficulty managing myself and my studies, but also like many academic autists, I made very few friends and had no idea how to endear myself to others. I still don't!

Graduation Day dawned at last. Lady students were expected to wear dresses in either black or white under their gowns, so I put on my white dress and draped myself in my black gown, hired as all gowns were in Aberdeen, where people who wore gowns at other times were looked on as pretentious at best and something unprintable at worst. My MA hood was also black and white, all very tasteful.

Although I'd studied at King's, that year all graduations took place at Marischal College in the centre of the city. It's world famous, one of the largest granite buildings in the world, and I'd hardly ever been in it before, but there was no difficulty finding my way in the stream of other black-and-white figures all around, laughing and chattering. I went in alone, but it didn't matter because we were all the same on that day, at that time, sharing in the same achievement.

Up to the platform we went, class by class in alphabetical order, to be tapped on the head with a mortar board (hat, not chunk of plywood!) and given a roll of ribbon-tied parchment, which we then gave back since the real certificates came out in the post. There was a ripple of laughter at my turn: the head-tapper had been bored into semi-unconsciousness by then and wasn't expecting someone almost a foot shorter than the average: he woke up abruptly and had to take a second swipe.

As I turned away I found my parents' faces in the crowd, and they were smiling. For the first time ever, I could see they weren't wondering why I was so unlike my smart, charming brother and what in the world to make of me. They weren't troubled about what out-of-joint thing I might say or do next. They were just glad and proud. So was everybody in the hall, everybody in the restaurant where we lunched, everybody in the photographer's. When I was walking back to the hire shop, passing the big townhouse where the courts are held, even a total stranger, a wee old man coming the other way, took in my outfit and called out, 'Well done, lass! Well done!'

So that's my definition of celebration. It's a time, however brief, when you fit. A period in life when the whole world around you is glad and you are exactly the same kind of glad. A magical moment in life when all the colours blend in harmony and nothing, not even I, can clash.

Armàda
Mòrag Law

Thàinig an Armàda beag againn fhìn anns an t-Sultain
aig an aon àm is a thàinig cuingealachaidhean Ìre a-Trì.
Madainn ghrianach nochd bhan mòr geal air beulaibh
an taighe le sgioba aighearach Spàinntich na broinn
– Mateo is Julia à Barcelona is dithis luchd-obraich
òga tapaidh à Ameireaga a Deas. Bha an uidheam
aca anns a' ghàrradh-cùl bhon là roimhe – spàidean
is sluasaidean, picichean is pocannan mòra saimeant
agus am measgaichear-saimeant fhathast na chadal gu
sàmhach fo tarpaulin. Gun dàil, thòisich na fir uile ga
chur air dòigh airson a' chiad là den obair le cabadaich is
gàireachdaich is fealla-dhà eatorra ann an Spàinntis.

Thàinig Julia don dhoras-cùl agus sheas i aig astar
sòisealta ceart airson bruidhinn rinn mu ar planaichean
airson a' ghàrraidh. 'S i bha modhail is dùrachdach
agus ged a bha coltas oirre mar deugaire beag caol
bha sùilean biorach, geurchùiseach aice is deagh fhios
againn gur i co-stiùiriche a' chompanaidh-ghàrraidh is
ise a' cumail smachd air a h-uile rud a-thaobh rianachd
is iomhais.

'A bheil sibh riaraichte gu leòr leis na planaichean?'
dh'fhaighnich i. 'Cuimhnichibh, ma tha dad sam bith
nach eil a' còrdadh ribh no ma tha sibh ag iarraidh
atharrachadh sam bith, fiù 's nuair a thòisicheas an
obair, leig fìos dhòmhsa air am fòn-làimh! Ged a tha
beagan Beurla aig Mateo, bidh e nas fhasa a' dèiligeadh
riumsa! Niste, bidh na leacan ùra airson an terras a'
ruighinn Dimàirt is am feansa ùr beagan às dèidh sin –
ach cumaidh mi fìos dhuibh, ma tha dàil ann.'

Às dèidh sin chaidh ise 's Mateo air falbh anns a' bhan agus nuair a thìll esan às a h-aonais bha na fir òga trang ag obair mu-thràth 's iad a' cladhach suas na seann leacan.

Agus b' e sin mar a bha e, fad dà mhìos. A h-uile là làn obair chorporra, chruaidh, na fir a' cladhach a-mach an t-seann talamh trom, ga chur ann am pocannan is an uair sin an toirt air falbh anns a' bhan. Bhiodh am measgaichear-saimeant a' tionndadh 's a shrann gun stad, 's na balaich a' tilgeil sluaiseadan làn pùdar-saimeant is gainmheach na chraos acrach. Lìon an àdhair mun cuairt orra le sgòthan salach dust is stùr, a' flòdraigeach air feadh a' ghàrraidh agus feum againn na h-uinneagan uile aig cùl an taighe a chumail dùinte. Cha do chùm sin fuaim a' chiùil aca a-mach, ge-tà, oir gu luath, nochd glaodhaire beag air mullach chruach bhriogaichean agus fhad 's a dh'obraich iad uile gu dripeil bha iad air am bogadh le ceòl aotrom, aighearach àrd. Òrain Spàinnteach le ruitheam is builleadh beòthail a thug blasad bhlàths an Costa del Sol do ar baile beag ciùin ann an Siorrachd Rinfriù. Anns na làithean mì-chìnnteach sin, thug e togail do ar cridheachan a bhith a' seasamh aig uinneag a' chidsin ag èisteachd ris a' cheòl is a'coimhead air sealladh a bha cho trang, cho adhartach is cho dòchasach.

Bha Mateo na dhuine beag fèitheach tapaidh is e a' stiùireadh an obair le siogarait beag cam daonnan na bheul, tiona tombaca is pacaid phàipearan-siogarait faisg air làimh. Thuig sinn sa bhad gum b' e clachair air leth sgileil a bh' ann cuideachd – a' tomhais 's a' còmharrachadh a-mach an terras is na frith-rathaidean ùra le sùil dhìreach is làmhan sgiobalta. Às dèidh seachdain, thòisich e air leacan an terras a chur sìos. Bhiodh e a' taghadh leac gu faiceallach agus an uair sin,

ag obair gu sgileil le a sgreadhail, bhiodh e a' sgaoileadh
còmhdach rèidh saimeant oirre. Chuireadh e sìos i na
h-àite cheart, ga gnogadh gu socair le cas an sgreadhail
is an uair sin ga tomhais a-rithist 's e a' dèanamh
cinnteach gu robh i còmhnard mus do thòisich e air an
ath tè. Às dèidh gach leac a chur sìos bhiodh e a' stad, a'
gabhail ceum air-ais 's a' coimhead oirre gu geur, 's e a'
gabhail ceò air a siogarait beag cam. Gu tric nuair a bha
e sàsaichte leis na rinn e bhiodh e a dèanamh ceum-
dannsa Spàinnteach no dhà, a' bualadh a bhasan san
àdhair mar dannsair Flamenco anns a bhriogais ghoirid
is leine-t còmhdaichte le pùdar-saimeant – a' sealltainn
gu foilleasach dè cho toilichte 's a bha e leis an obair-
chuird aige-fhèin.

Abair gun do dh'obraich an sgioba Spàinnteach
againn gu cruaidh fad dà mhìos – is Julia a' nochdadh
gu cunbhalach cuideachd airson sùil a chumail air an
adhartas. Gu slaodach, mionaideach dh'èirich cumadh
a' ghàrraidh ùir le ballachan beaga mun cuairt an terras
agus frith-rathaidean lùbte rèidh. Mu dheireadh thall
cha robh ach na feansaichean ùra rin togail is am feur
ùr ri chur sìos. B' e deireadh na Dàmhair a bh' ann
a-nis is na làithean a' fàs na b' fhuaire is na bu ghiorra.
Air an là mu dheireadh is feum aca air pròiseact mòra
ann an sgìre eile a thòiseachadh an ath-là, thàinig
an obair gu crìoch le a bhith a' cur sìos am feur is a'
sgioblachadh suas anns an leth-dorchadas. B' e am fuaim
mu dheireadh a chuala sinn brùnsgal a' mheasgaichear-
saimeant 's iad ga roiligeadh air falbh airson a chur
anns a' bhan mhòr gheal. Rinn iad dùdanach dhuinn
's iad a' draibheadh sìos an sràid dhorcha shàmhach,
mar chomharra gu robh an Armàda fo siùil a-rithist, a'
dèanamh a cùrsa gu costaichean ùra.

Gu h-obann bha an gàrradh deiseil ach a' laighe

falamh is sàmhach, às aonais cabadaich beòthail is ceòl àrd Spàinnteach. Mhair an sgìre againne ann an Ìre a-Trì gus àm na Nollaig 's an uair sin thàinig Ìre a-Ceithir agus, aig toiseach na Bliadhna Ùir, an dàrna Ghlasadh.

Anns a' Ghearran thàinig an sneachd mar phlangaid tiugha geal a' còmhdachadh a' ghàrraidh slàn ach bha aiteamh ann aig a cheart àm a fhuair sinn ar ciad bhanachdaichean. Agus air madainn tràth san Earrach sheas sinn aig uinneag a' chidsin a' coimhead air lòn-dubh air mullach an fheansa ùir, sruth phongan ceòlmhor cridheil a' dòrtadh às a ghob soilleir buidhe 's e a' dèanamh gàirdeachas ann an solas na grèine.

Armada

Our little Armada arrived in September, just as the Level 3 restrictions began. On a sunny morning a large white van drew up outside the house, carrying a lively crew of Spaniards – Mateo and Julia from Barcelona, along with two sturdy young labourers from South America. Their equipment had been left in the back garden the previous day – spades, shovels and picks, big bags of cement and the cement-mixer, still peacefully asleep under its tarpaulin cover. The men immediately set to work, getting everything prepared for the first day's work, chattering, laughing and joking in Spanish.

Julia came round to the back door to discuss our plans for the garden, standing at the regulation social distance. She was very serious and respectful, and although she looked like just a slip of a girl, her eyes were sharp and shrewd and we were already aware that she was the co-director of the landscaping company, in charge of all the administration and finance.

'Are you satisfied with the plans?' she asked. 'Remember, if there's anything at all that you would like to change, even once the work gets underway, just give me a phone! Although Mateo speaks a little English it'll be easier to deal with me. Now, the slabs for the terrace will be arriving on Monday and your new fence will come a little later – but I'll let you know if there's going to be any delay.'

After that, she and Mateo disappeared in the van and when he returned alone, the two young labourers had already begun to dig up the old paving-slabs.

And that's how it was, for the next two months. Each day was filled with hard, physical labour as the men dug up all the old, heavy soil then put it into bags for taking away in the van. The cement-mixer hummed and spun incessantly as the two lads threw shovelfuls of sand and powdered cement into its hungry maw. The air around them was hazy with gritty clouds of dust which floated across the whole garden, meaning that we had to keep all the windows at the back of the house tight shut. However, that didn't stop the sound of their music, amplified by a little speaker balanced on a pile of bricks. While they toiled away, they were immersed in loud Spanish pop songs whose lively beat and rhythm brought the warmth of the Costa del Sol to our sedate Renfrewshire village. In those uncertain days it lifted our hearts to stand at the kitchen window, listening to the music and looking at the busy, forward-looking, hopeful scene unfolding in front of us.

Mateo was a muscular, sturdy little man. He would direct operations with a squint little roll-up in the corner of his mouth, his tin of tobacco and packet of cigarette-papers always close at hand. We soon realised just what a skilled stonemason he was, measuring and marking out the new paths and terrace with neat hands and keen eyes. After a week, he began to lay the new slabs for the terrace. He would choose a slab very carefully and then, skilfully wielding his trowel, would spread a smooth layer of cement on it. He would then position it accurately, tapping it gently with the handle of the trowel to make sure it was level, before starting on the next one. Before continuing, he would pause, take a step back and check his handiwork, puffing thoughtfully on his little roll-up. It was quite obvious how much enjoyment his craftsmanship gave him, for often after laying a slab he would perform a few Spanish dance-steps, clapping his hands in the air like a flamenco dancer in his shorts and dusty T-shirt.

How hard our Spanish crew worked over those two months, with regular visits from Julia too, to keep an eye on progress. Slowly and precisely, the shape of the new garden began to emerge, with little walls round the new terrace and smooth, curved paths. Finally, all that was left to do was erect the fence and lay fresh turf. By now it was late October and the days were getting colder and shorter. On the very last day, with the start-date for the next big project imminent, the work finally ended with the turf being laid and the big tidy-up being done in the half-darkness. The last sound we heard was the rumble of the cement-mixer as they rolled it away to be put in the van, then they tooted the horn as they drove off down the quiet, empty street – signalling that our Armada was under sail again, heading for other shores.

All of a sudden, our garden was finished but lying empty and silent with no lively chatter or loud Spanish music. Our area remained in Level 3 till Christmas time, followed by Level 4 and then the second lockdown.

In February it snowed, covering the whole garden with a thick white blanket, but the thaw came at exactly the same time as we received our first vaccinations. And, one morning in early spring, we stood at the kitchen window watching a blackbird on the new fence, rejoicing in the morning sun, a stream of heartfelt notes pouring from his bright yellow beak.

Friday Night Treat
Simon Lamb

What am I having for dinner tonight?
Shall I celebrate Friday with Angel Delight?
Shall I order a pizza or maybe a curry,
or noodles or sushi? But I needn't worry,
'cause there's only one meal that I want to eat,
and that's a fish 'n' chip supper as a Friday night treat!

Slip-quick as a flash, I'm off out to the chippy,
togged up in my jacket 'cause it's Scotland and nippy,
and then I am there and I'm stood in the queue
with my eyes to the skies on a bullet-point menu
with hundreds of options, but my love's unconditional
for the first on the list: I'm going traditional.

I want fish! I want fish! I want chips and more chips!
I want salt! I want vinegar! I'm licking my lips
as it's wrapped in a bag ('Help yersel' tae a fork!'),
but by then I am out and I'm walking the walk
down the streets to the shore of the town where I'm
from,
and I'm drawn like a magnet to the arms of the prom,

where the sea and the sky are a-trysting in blue,
so wide and so deep, and I drink in the view,
and I nestle between with my parcel, my treat,
as the sun takes its leave. Not a person I meet.
The harbour is quiet. Not a breath from the boats.
Silence from Hawick to John o' Groats.

Then I open the bag, and I open up love,
and out comes the food and the stars up above
start to glimmer and shimmer in tastebuddy glee
at the sight of the fish and the chips on my knee,
'cause the universe knows and understands
that it's not just a meal that's here in my hands:

it's more, so much more; it's a memory, you see.
It's a big little thing, this Friday night tea,
and it's big little things that warm us inside,
like a fish 'n' chip supper that's enjoyed by the tide.
So I eat and I look and I look and I eat,
giving thanks to the world for each Friday night treat,

and with mouthfuls delicious, I vow to hold dear
the gift of knowing that I was here,
beside the sea, beneath the sky,
at one with the world with my Friday night fry.
Aye, there's no better feeling, I guarantee,
than fish 'n' chips in your lap down the prom for your
tea.

Author note: *My poem is inspired by many joyous
fish 'n' chip suppers enjoyed down the prom, none more
so than one particular night in Wick, Caithness, with
winter approaching, and feeling this incredible sense of
'I am here', a celebration of being alive, and all from the
simple pleasure of warm food and a warm heart.*

Celebrate
Courtney Stoddart

for me, writing is a form of celebration
I love to express my thoughts on the page
written or typed it fills my heart with joy
there is little to celebrate these days
these days, I feel a weight on my chest
it's heavy.
it's always lurking, peeking behind curtains
while my other selves roam fancy-free

I know there are forests
but I can't see them for the trees
I feel the weight of tyranny downpressing me
but when I pick up my pen and write
the words become my fire to see me through the night –
resistance
I am writing my existence into reality
like a map laid out for me
pen in hand, I write to erase the rules and formalities
which keep us bound
there are tethered hounds which howl at the wolves I see
these rebel wolves are still hounding me to join their
pack
they tell me that if I want to be free I have to ride like
Natty Dread and attack
I think back, to when I was young
I always wanted to be part of the popular crew and
parrot references
to what was cool and have my peers left in awe and
deference too

but now my reverence, my celebration
is for those who stand up to systems of segregation
even when it's not popular to say what needs saying
for the sake of liberation
I celebrate the greats whose words tore down nations
heading for damn nation
I say damn this nation
I feel I'm suffocating so I have to find a breath for
celebration
and sometimes it's like finding needles in haystacks of
discrimination

we wear our chains with pride and we think we're free
like ghosts we're haunting the people we should really
be
I want to celebrate but I can't shake the shackles from
my feet
I dance anyway, I stomp my souls into the earth
and I pray for the release, I want to celebrate
so I tell my loved ones how much they mean to me
they're my soil, and they give life to my tree
I'm a renegade, but trust and connection is my ultimate
need
so I celebrate the ones who bring comfort to me
our affinity, is the reason I sing every morning
the reason I become like lightning storming if I hear of
anyone
any state or any structure trying to do harm to their
good hearts
because I am so adoring of their good hearts
in admiration of the wisdom they impart
and despite the harsh nights
they carry on with love and with light
that's why I celebrate

'cause if I forget how to love then I have become nothing
and I am of no use to anyone or anything
so don't forget to celebrate, rest and restore
in the hard times and the good
behold a pale horse
only celebration could make death take down his hood
and drop his torch
celebration is to humanity what a fire is to wood
so of course –
celebration is a cleansing force

A Celebration of a Life

Jane Swanson

A sudden peal of celebratory bells rings out loud
and clear from the tower of St Peter's Church. It's an
unexpected sound, something I haven't heard in a long
time. Joyful, majestic cascading arcs of music spill out
high above the town. I wait to see if a wedding party
appears at the open door, but there's no one around,
and I wonder if another event like an anniversary or
an ordination is being celebrated inside the church. A
gentle spasm of longing eases across my shoulders. The
last time I heard a bell ringing was in the radiotherapy
department of a hospital, a large brass bell like a ship's
bell with a blue rope that rang out to salute the end of a
long course of treatment. The bell had a deep, metallic
clang, and moments afterwards, when it was silent,
there was a hush in the waiting room, a silence that
complemented the bell as a poignant marker of the
event. I am struck by how the sound of that bell lies
deeply rooted in my memory. When I think about it, I
realise that bells have provided a soundtrack to many
significant moments in my life.

All over the world the sound of ringing bells brings
people together. Bells call out for our celebrations and
toll with compassion for our grief and sadness. With the
sound of celebration vibrating through the air I sit down
on a bench opposite the church door, straighten my
shoulders and take the time to quietly celebrate all the
precious moments in my life that have been marked by
the sound of ringing bells...

The dull, cold clank of the hand bell rung by the teacher in the schoolyard is my earliest memory of hearing a bell. They were happy, carefree days with scuffed knees, whirling skipping ropes and endless games of marbles.

There was the sprightly chime of the old-fashioned shop bell on a rusted steel spring above the door of my grandmother's dress shop, as sprightly and cheery as the way she sprang up from her chair behind the counter to greet her customers.

The first album I bought in 1973 was *Tubular Bells*, by Mike Oldfield; the many changes of mood in this instrumental piece chimed perfectly with the complex emotions I experienced as a teenager. The music begins with a soft tempo, an eerie sound, and builds as more percussion instruments acoustically weave their way into the composition. The steely, resonant sound of the tubular bells being struck with a hammer sounded like the hand bells we played in the music department at school.

The tintinnabulation of bells on my wedding day singing out from the top of the church spire. Bells pulled by bell ringers who heaved on ropes attached to wooden wheels, so that the bells swung open-mouthed through full circles and rang out in jubilant rounds.

The jingle of wooden hand-held sleigh bells at the many shows at my children's school; the clink-clink of the tiny brass bells sewn onto their red Santa hats on Christmas morning, and the clattering-clap of shiny cowbells they bought as holiday souvenirs.

The brittle sound of the ancient church bell ringing in the cool air during a stay at Lluc Monastery in the Serra de Tramuntana mountains in the north-west of Mallorca; the deep, sonorous hum of a vibrating Tibetan singing bowl, and the chink-chink of tingsha bells at the beginning and end of a yoga class. Spiritual bells that over the years have settled my mind, helped me reflect on life, to find peace and an ease of being.

The crystalline tinkling sound of the cut-glass bell my mother kept on her bedside table and would ring when my parents needed help in the night.

The slow, repeated clangour of a solitary tenor bell at my parents' funerals when we gave thanks and commemorated their lives.

The bells of St Peter's fall silent, a resonant hum lingers in the air, I look up at the tower and can't help but smile.

Author note: *The unexpected sound of church bells ringing out with joy in my home town.*